Country Enterprise

ALREADY PUBLISHED

Growing Fuchsias
K. Jennings and V. Miller

Growing Hardy Perennials
Kenneth A. Beckett

Growing Dahlias
Philip Damp

Growing Irises
G.E. Cassidy and S. Linnegar

Growing Cyclamen
Gay Nightingale

Violets
Roy E. Coombs

Climbing Plants
Kenneth A. Beckett

Plant Hunting in Nepal
Roy Lancaster

The History of Gardens
Christopher Thacker

Better Gardening
Robin Lane Fox

Slipper Orchids
Robin Graham with Ronald Roy

Growing Chrysanthemums
Harry Randall and Alan Wren

The Rock Gardener's Handbook
Alan Titchmarsh

Waterlilies
Philip Swindells

IN PREPARATION

The Pelargonium Species
William J. Webb

Wine Growing in England
J.G. Barrett

1000 Decorative Plants
J.L. Krempin

Victorians and their Flowers
Nicolette Scourse

The Salad Garden
Elizabeth Arter

Growing Lilies
D.B. Fox

The Cottage Garden Year
Roy Genders

Growing Begonias
E. Catterall

Growing Bulbs
Martyn Rix

Growing Roses
Michael Gibson

The Water Gardener's Handbook
Philip Swindells

Country Enterprise

Pleasure and Profit from Home Produce

JONATHAN and HEATHER FFRENCH

CROOM HELM
London & Canberra

©1983 Jonathan and Heather Ffrench
Croom Helm Ltd, Provident House, Burrell Row,
Beckenham, Kent BR3 1AT

British Library Cataloguing in Publication Data

Ffrench, Jonathan
    Country enterprise.
    1. Small business — Great Britain   2. Great
Britain — Rural conditions
    I. Title   II. Ffrench, Heather
338.6'42'0941   HD2346.G7

ISBN 0-7099-1034-7

Printed and bound in Great Britain

Contents

1. Analysing Your Assets / 1
2. Land Use / 10
3. Vegetables / 22
4. Soft Fruit Growing / 37
5. The Flower Garden and the Herb Garden / 46
6. The Orchard and the Vineyard / 55
7. Woodlands / 60
8. Sheep / 69
9. Beef / 82
10. Pigs / 86
11. Rabbits / 97
12. Hens / 100
13. Ducks / 112
14. Geese / 119
15. Dairying / 125
16. The Kitchen / 140
17. Kitchen Recipes / 145
18. Bees / 172
19. Wool / 184
20. Water / 189
21. Marketing and Selling / 194
22. Finance / 211
Index / 214

Analysing Your Assets

To achieve success in any enterprise you must have certain assets. In some fields, such as opera singing, you require only yourself, in a healthy state. If you wish to keep a hundred head of deer, you require at least a hundred acres of land, surrounded by a fence at least six feet high. Between the two extremes there is a multitude of possibilities for country enterprises. At the very simplest you can make country-style produce, buying in all the raw materials and producing it in an urban kitchen or shed. You could make delicious raspberry jam from berries bought in a street market or you could make traditional furniture using wood bought from a do-it-yourself supermarket and polished with your own concoction of turpentine and beeswax (you can buy the beeswax, you do not even have to keep the bees). If you have a variety of buildings at your disposal, say a few stables and a pole barn, your choice of enterprise widens to include the possibility of keeping livestock. Without the buildings but with a little land you can produce vegetables or fruit and keep bees and some chickens. With a lot of land and buildings you have the widest choice of enterprises. This probably makes the choice all the more difficult; choice is easiest when you have only a few options.

However, there is one requirement that is constant in all these situations. You have to want to do something yourself and you have to be able to do what you want. The first step has to be to analyse your own abilities. The easiest bit of the analysis is to decide on your physical abilities. If you are strong, do you like using your strength? If you do, then pursue an enterprise where strength is valuable. Many forms of workshop production, such as tanning and woodworking, are easier if you are strong and in livestock enterprises where the animals are bulky (suckler cows, for example), it is useful to be able to carry sacks full of feed with ease when lesser mortals would struggle. If your strength is limited, use your gentler touch for keeping bees or rabbits, or growing lightweight crops, salads or flowers. Spinning from a raw fleece is satisfying and a true craft.

Having decided on the sort of enterprise to which you are most suited, the next stage is to analyse where you intend to carry out the enterprise. With the urban kitchen or shed the choices are fairly clear: cooking in one, woodwork, pottery and other bench crafts in the other. Spinning only occupies a space some four feet square and weaving not much more, depending on the size of loom. These are all traditional country-style occupations from which you can earn money in an urban setting. The most shabby-looking buildings are valuable if they suit the enterprise you have in mind. Sheep like plenty of ventilation if housed; hay and straw can be stored in not much more than a roof on legs. Cattle also thrive in fresh air if you have room to keep them. With solid buildings, like stables, solid-sided barns and so on, the choice of enterprise increases to include pig- or poultry-keeping. Some buildings make the choice easy. We bought a property once with a pig farm on it. There was a farrowing house (a maternity unit), pens for the sows and fattening pens for porkers. To build that from scratch would have cost us more than we paid for the house and buildings so the asset was extremely valuable to us. When we sold the house and pig farm many years later the new owner knocked the whole lot down because the asset had no value for him. We just wished we could have transported the buildings. A dairy or similar building has beautifully lined walls, it is ideal for milk or other food production, drains will have been laid to carry water well away — that is assuming, of course, that whoever constructed the dairy did as they were meant to. Even the dirtiest old dairies tend to respond miraculously to some tender loving care and a great deal of soap and water.

If you have a range of glasshouses then their value is dependent on their condition. Acres and acres of glasshouses have fallen into disrepair. Almost inevitably it is then cheaper to pull them all down and erect polytunnels. Having said that, it is cheaper still simply to put the polytunnels on virgin land. Old greenhouses are more often a liability than an asset. With a great many buildings of all sorts of shapes and sizes your choice is governed by the land, if any, that you also have. Many enterprises with livestock can be carried out without land whereas some, like sheep-keeping, are really only practicable if there is land in the summer. Of course, the land does not have to be with the buildings. Many sheep and cattle farmers rent land to which they travel to check their livestock. With a lot of land and buildings you can either separate the two, running intensive livestock in the buildings and farming the land, or you can use the buildings with the land, for inwintering livestock and so on.

Waiting Assets — Empty Buildings

If you decide to carry on an enterprise in a property in which you already live, go outside on a rainy day, look around you and decide quite truthfully what you would like to be doing. If the answer is honestly that you would be happy out there working then your choice remains open. If the answer is that you would much rather be indoors reading the paper then under no circumstances be tempted into keeping livestock. Things that can escape, and anything that can walk, fly or swim will escape on wet days. Wet, windy or the most awkward day that you can imagine. That is when the sheep 'go walkies' or the fox gets in with the geese and they start flapping all over the county. Almost everybody with livestock has had somebody let something out, whether accidentally or deliberately. We have had ponies let out on Christmas night by over-merry revellers. We have had sheep escape through gaps forced through hedges by over-enthusiastic walkers. It is all part of life's rich tapestry but if the thought of an unexpected interruption in a working day fills you with horror, then it is a part of the tapestry you would be better without. Keeping livestock means that seven days a week are working days. Even if you are not having to feed the animal or bird concerned, you must still keep a constant eye on it. Sheep happily grazing in an immaculately fenced field may look as if they can be left for a week or two. Apart from the fact that the law requires you to check on your animals daily, there is the sad fact that animals do become sick or injured and if left to their own devices die remarkably quickly.

Growing enterprises — vegetables, fruit or other crops — can often be left for short periods during the year. Enterprises like jam-making are spasmodic unless your market requires a regular service. We find that we have a mad peak of activity in the soft fruit season when many of our customers are catering for a tourist trade. One of the advantages our customers have is that we will make up orders on a rush basis. Sometimes it becomes hectic but it means that our customers appreciate our efforts and give us the valuable business in times of low demand. With any seasonal enterprise the problem is of a frantic activity and then a lull. This is another factor to consider when choosing your enterprise: the time of year when you want to be the most active. We have various peaks. The jam in the summer, geese for Christmas and there is always a flurry in pork around Easter. Spring is also busy with lambs and growth starting on the land. With any enterprise that involves land use, the traditional 'dead' time after Christmas is filled with necessary repair work to drives, ditches and fences. The important thing if you are relying on your enterprise to support you financially is either to have made enough in the busy months to cover the gap or to be producing something that sells through this period. In general, livestock that is fattened on the land is sold off the grass at the end of the summer. If you keep the animals through to January, you will have had to feed them expensive concentrates. Laying birds will produce an income through this time and any enterprise that is run intensively, such as pigs, can be timed to show a return now. Speciality vegetables are mainly summer crops, apart from forced roots such as chicory. The more traditional vegetables that are available at this time of year are often low-priced ones such as the humble carrot. A dairy enterprise will be producing an income unless you have goats that are about to kid and unless you have chosen to have cows dry at this time. Crafted items such as hand-spun wool are best sold before Christmas and in the summer in tourist areas. In the country enterprise then, the age-old tradition of the winter being a time to survive on the fat you made in the summer seems still to apply. This is another asset you must produce to survive any business that has seasonal peaks and troughs.

If your enterprise is simply planned as an extra to another income, then of course the seasonal aspect of earning can make the whole process even more satisfying. What could be nicer than a good bonus from your craft work just before Christmas. A good extra income from summer produce could perhaps pay for a late holiday. The main aim if this is your enterprise must be that you do not commit yourself to something that means you can never get away to enjoy the fruits of your success. There are various ways of arranging this. Sometimes you can find a friend who will look after your livestock when you are away in return for similar assistance from you. If it is a question of leaving growing crops, then as long as you time it correctly you only need someone to keep a vague eye on things. We once had the builder who was working on our house look after our pigs while we went away for a weekend. To our astonishment, he volunteered when he heard our normal back-up was unavailable. As it turned out he had had pigs himself some years ago and the whole arrangement worked very well. We paid him in pork at his request! So that is another asset to consider, having someone who can stand in if need be.

Sometimes you can buy an asset with a property — not simply the buildings or land but perhaps a wood. There is a chapter on woodland that helps to classify what kind of wood it is. It may be an area of water (there is a chapter on that too). Even strange things like wind power can be seen as an asset in some ways. Wind-powered electricity storage systems can save on heating and lighting costs and in many enterprises this can make an appreciable difference. If you live near the sea, you may well have access to plentiful seaweed and this is a tremendous fertiliser for vegetables and fruit. If you live in the very heart of a city, you have a potential market all around you so if you can produce a marketable product you can succeed. You can even keep livestock in high-rise flats by keeping bees on a balcony (as long as your landlord agrees). Hives are kept on some office roofs and town honey-producers are often winners at honey shows. Bees will travel to collect their nectar. When London and other cities still had areas of bomb damage the bee population must have been especially content: masses of the pink weed — rose bay willow herb — quickly clothed the bomb site. Often referred to as 'fireweed' it grows in profusion on fire-razed ground. In town and country it shows the position of fires long gone. Its sweet nectar is a great favourite with bees.

Country enterprises started off life as we know it today. After all the person who was good at making pots soon became the village potter. The person who was good at transforming wood into usable objects formed his own business. Whether these enterprises received payment in kind or in money makes very little difference; it was still a case of an enterprising individual able to use his assets to the best of his ability and the market-place accepting that he had something acceptable with which to trade.

The final assets required to succeed in a country enterprise are the ability and determination to sell your product. This is very often the biggest stumbling-block. Unless you accept from the outset that what you produce must one day be sold, you are not going to receive any income from your venture. The thought of producing enough to eat and drink for your family from your own resources became immensely popular a few years ago. The independence to be gained was seen as a worthwhile goal and certainly home-produced food is extremely nutritious. The drawback to the concept is that unfortunately in our modern world we have to produce a surprising amount of cash to survive. Rates, rent or mortgage payments cannot be made with honey; even if you burn wood to heat your house and fuel your cooker, you will still probably appreciate electric light and if you aim to live well on your home-grown produce, then a deep-freeze is a great help. Also many people were so good at producing to feed themselves that they produced gluts that needed to be disposed of. This leads on naturally to producing extra especially to sell. The satisfaction we felt when we first sold our hand-raised pies to local pubs and restaurants still glows today. The pork in them was home-produced as was the lard in the pastry. There is a tremendous amount of pleasure to be had from this kind of venture. There are, of course, always bad days. The hurt you feel if someone criticises your produce is unbelievable until you have felt it. Even if you can see that the criticism is unfounded and that the customer is just letting off steam, it will probably haunt you at night. That is one of the problems of working with such personal projects: the satisfaction is tremendous on good days but bad days are worse than you can imagine. An essential asset is to be able to ride them. Information about marketing and selling can be found in Chapter 21.

When you produce a specialist product you want it to reach the market for which it is intended and it is worth taking a lot of trouble to make sure that it does. Many retailers enjoy buying from 'the chap who makes it'. We produce a wholegrain mustard and however many different people we have used to sell it, it is always when we go out ourselves that the sales go up. It is natural after all. We can comment on how it is made and it means that the shopkeeper can tell his customers that it is a special product that came straight from the mixing bowl to the jar to the shop. This is another piece of essential self-analysis before you choose an enterprise. If you simply cannot bear the thought of going out and selling your produce yourself, then choose something which has an established market. Sheep, cattle and pigs can be sold through a local market and you do not have to be there at all. With more involved produce such as cheese and fudges, someone must actually sell it for you. Advertising for salesmen for this kind of small-scale project is a nightmare. Very few people want to start up an operation. Established delivery rounds are quite a different matter. We have tried agents who actually advertised for small lines but unfortunately most of them hang on to your stock for ages and certainly do not put much effort into selling it. If you are lucky you may have a friend who is the ideal person, in which case approach him before you produce anything, then if he says 'no' —

at least you are not left to eat half a ton of fudge yourselves! Quite often you have potential customers all around you. If you work in an office or have family and friends that do, this can be an excellent source of business. We sold pork joints to a factory for years. It became a routine on the last Friday of every month that legs and loins and the occasional half-pig were avidly disposed of. Unfortunately that factory is now closed but if you can find a contact like that, you do not have to go out looking for the business, it comes to you.

Farm gate sales are another way that people come to you to buy. With a delightful property in the country, on a busy road, a nicely worded sign will have you instantly in business. If the road is busy enough you can even dispense with the delightful property; if the property is delightful enough people will beat a path to your door if you encourage them enough. In a suburban setting you may have the planning officials beating a path to your door if the whole approach is too enthusiastic. At least in suburbia and in town you do not have to go so far to find potential customers.

The method of packaging and design that you choose depends to a great extent on the area in which you intend to sell. In an urban environment, people may well buy produce that looks as if it comes from the country but they will probably expect the label to look formal. In other words, you will have to have a label composed of formal lettering at least. In a country setting, a more informal layout is often successful. Often produce such as jam and fudge is bought by tourists and they certainly demand originality, something that they would not expect to buy at home. Tourists in this sense are rarely people who are actually staying in your area. Often the best sales of rural goods are to people on afternoon drives or short weekends. Where we live in Kent, the tourist season is strictly April to October. This is because these are the opening times for the local stately homes. It is worth analysing the activity of transitory buyers where you intend to sell. In an office environment, for example, there are peaks at bank holidays, Christmas and Easter. In the summer, people are away on holiday and you do not have a peak.

Eventually someone has to do the bookkeeping for the enterprise. Retailers will certainly want receipts and you may find yourself involved in VAT. A simple method is usually the most effective, unless of course you are an accountant going into chickens in which case it would be a good idea to produce a simple clear booklet on the subject for everyone else to follow. It is astonishing how dynamic entrepreneurs go to pieces over 'the books'. We have eventually decided after much trial and error and a continual endeavour to switch responsibility from one to the other that the only answer is to compile figures daily. It only takes a few minutes and becomes part of a routine. However, we still find that this is the most arduous part of the whole enterprise.

Land Use

GRASS

Grass provides food for animals that in turn provide food for us. On the other hand, on a domestic scale, it requires eradicating from patios and, if we encourage the lawn to grow by using fertilisers, we complain when we have to cut it. Agricultural grass is not usually berated for growing too enthusiastically, unless of course it is growing as a weed in another crop. The aim is generally to grow as good grass as is possible on a given area and then feed it as effectively as possible to an animal that will convert it into meat or milk or simply into more animals. This kind of grassland falls into one of two basic categories: permanent pasture or new leys.

PERMANENT PASTURE

There are 5M hectares of permanent pasture in Britain. Often this is found on banks and slopes that it would be impossible to cultivate regularly by machine. Much pasture on steep slopes and hills, however picturesque, is poor in food value. It provides grazing for deer, sheep and some cattle. The grasses are mainly fescues and bents. This kind of pasture needs constant grazing to prevent it from returning to its natural state of growing sedges, heather and bracken. Even real moorland, covered in heather and bracken, requires some management to maintain its value. Now that labour is being reduced on many moors and gamekeepers no longer regularly burn the heather to keep the growth down, fires take a disastrous hold. The leggy heather stalks fuel a raging fire that burns right through the underlying peat itself. This leaves only bare rocks and stones and provides no foothold at all for grasses. This reduces the moor's capacity for grazing sheep and deer and also alters the landscape.

Country Jigsaw

Good permanent pasture consists mainly of ryegrass and clover. It can also be picturesque — Constable-type landscapes with slow-flowing rivers. The surrounding fields were once rich with cowslips, orchids and chirruping grasshoppers. Today many of the grasshoppers have been exterminated. The high cost of land requires heavy stocking on summer grazing. Thick grass growth means no bare patches in the sward. This deprives the grasshopper of the open area it requires in the egglaying stage of its life cycle. So gradually the grasshoppers fall prey to our intensive use of the land. Our forbears used to graze their animals heavily into the autumn using up the last of the cheapest feedstuff, grass. We no longer do this as grazing to the roots can impair next year's grass crop. This means that winter light does not reach the low-lying leaf rosettes of field weeds such as green-winged orchids and cowslips. These plants manufacture much of their food during Winter and early Spring. No light: no cowslips, and so our landscape changes again.

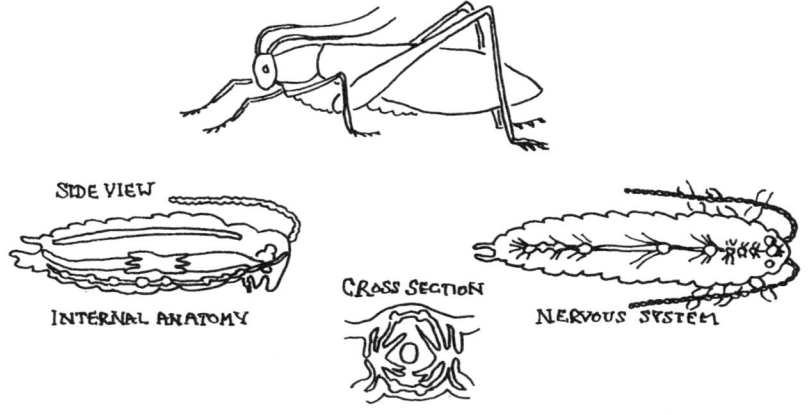

a complex piece of natural engineering that is falling victim to intensive farming

The Longhorn Grasshopper

Permanent pasture can be improved by harrowing and scarifying to spread unevenly deposited dung and remove dead matter clogging the roots. Many of the fields used for grazing today would once have been reserved for hay; they would then have been referred to as meadows and those that carried stock were called pasture. Probably the meadows would have been grazed after the hay was cut. The concept of cutting only hay from an expensive acre of ground is not often practised today.

NEW LEYS

This is grassland that is sown, grazed and maintained for a few years and is then dug up. This increases the potential growth of grass in an area. Permanent weeds are simpler to eradicate and the newest high-yielding grass seeds can be sown. New leys can be planted continuously on the same field or alternatively a grass crop can provide a break in an arable rotation. It is, of course, possible to grow the grass simply as a green crop to plough back in to enrich the land. Generally, however, stock are put on to it to graze, their dung manuring the land and the animals growing to provide a cash crop.

Different species of grass peak at differing times so if you are planting new grass in three fields you could choose different varieties. This will spread your work load at hay- or silage-making. The first and main cut for hay and silage is taken between 20 May and 14 June; this is the finest quality grass and cuts taken later in the year are not usually so nutritious. In any case, hay must always be cut before the stalks become too thick and fibrous. You can feed your hay to your own stock or sell it. If you live in a 'horsey' area, good hay will be at a premium. Small pets like guinea-pigs also consume hay and it is often worth bagging a few pounds of hay into polythene bags for sale to this market. The 'mark up' on hay sold this way is often staggering: a pet shop near us appears to be making something like 1,000 per cent profit on the little bags of hay! Clearly the guinea-pig owner does not want a whole bale, his pet would probably take over a year to eat it. If you can sell your bags Farm Gate you could afford to charge half the pet shop's charge and still make an inflated profit. It is being said that the traditional oblong bale will become a thing of the past. The giant roller bales that are carried around on tractors mounted with fearsome spikes are apparently going to take over. That is all very well if you want to move your hay and straw only by machine. There are still a lot of instances, such as near horses and in awkward old buildings, where the tractor would be a nuisance. Still perhaps one day we will consider the oblong bale as much a speciality product as the pet bag. One thing that would be avoided is all the itching you get from carrying a bale on your back as you stagger across the yard, frantically clutching a pail of water in your free hand. Such feats of strength are usually inspired by trying to dash through evening feed before going out on a Saturday evening. The main problem is that like that famous lager, dried thistles itch parts of you that other plants cannot reach!

Silage is never clutched close to you while being carried about, its smell is far too lingering. Silage is really pickled grass, as sauerkraut is pickled cabbage. The grass is compressed without air, often an additive stabilises the process and the grass preserves itself in its own juice. To live near your own silage clamp is acceptable, you breathe in the odour and picture your animals growing contentedly. To live near someone else's silage heap is another thing altogether: you get all of the drawbacks with none of the profit. The newest method of silage-making is to put giant roller bales into heavyweight polythene sacks. This way the silage is easily transported still in its wrapper and the farmer avoids having to construct a special silage clamp. There have been one or two teething problems with this method, the most shattering of these to a sleepy farmer is that some of the bags have exploded with a sound like a rifle shot. These explosions have burst the bags which ruins the silage (unless it is ready, in which case you can feed it straight away), but hopefully they have not caused too many alarms.

Silage does not always work. Successful silage is itself an acquired odour but silage gone wrong is even worse. Years ago we experimented with putting grass into redundant fertiliser bags. We were aiming to make silage in small quantities for our goats. It was decidedly a hit or miss affair. If you opened a dud bag, you smelt awful for days. The goats were not dreadfully enthusiastic about the project but sheep love silage. A large ewe carrying twins will consume up to 5.5 kg a day. This can form her whole diet but she may find it difficult in late pregnancy to eat this quantity, as the lambs will not leave enough food inside her, so she will need concentrates towards the end of the pregnancy. Cattle love silage and thrive on it. Silage effluent, the liquid that drains off from the clamp, used to be viewed as an extremely toxic problem to dispose of. It is certainly very toxic in rivers and waterways. It is twice as potent as pig slurry, another liquid problem. When the effluent enters rivers the highly soluble organic nutrients and minerals it contains give a phenomenal boost to the natural microbe population. These multiply rapidly and so deplete the dissolved oxygen in the water, with the result that the resident fish population dies of suffocation. Considerable work has now gone into investigating silage effluent and it has been found that when stabilised, it forms an admirable food for livestock. Pigs love it and will consume large quantities daily as will cattle. It now appears that a major pollution problem has a happy answer. After all no-one is going to let a valuable crop flow down into rivers.

FERTILISATION OF GRASSLAND

Grassland has been limed for centuries — even if you aim to produce organically, its use is approved. If the grass in your fields requires lime then it will not produce a worthwhile crop without it. What else you do to your fields is up to your judgement and beliefs. If your aim is to produce every single blade of grass that your land can possibly yield than you must use nitrogen. Some fields can consume vast quantities of it. You must also add phosphorus and potassium, bearing in mind that too much potassium can limit magnesium uptake (if you graze sheep and cows this can lead to an attack of staggers). It is certainly worth having your soil analysed and then working out very carefully what to add, unless, of course, you start to feel that the whole exercise is creating too much 'chemistry lesson' type of involvement. In that case, 'go organic' although you must still fertilise the grass, that is keep on with the lime and apply farm yard manure with a generous hand.
    There is growing concern that the overuse of chemicals exhausts the land. It certainly reduces the number of earthworms, those wriggly friends that do an effective job of deep ploughing for you. For these reasons, some farmers only use organically based fertilisers on their land. Although the chemical content of the fertiliser varies at times, great claims are made for its effectiveness. Farm yard manure is an essential by-product of animal husbandry, unless, of course, you keep your animals on concrete without bedding or on slats. The concrete-without-bedding saga is becoming a welfare issue. There is probably going to be action to make it compulsory to give tethered pigs bedding. If you see pigs tethered to the spot on bare flooring you will hopefully feel a mad urge to

give the poor creatures some straw. Pigs love cosy beds. Running pigs on a slatted floor is different, the floors are often constructed to feel warm to the touch — well, at least warmer than concrete. We still like to see our happy pigs on their straw beds so we are enthusiastic FYM producers. It is wonderfully powerful stuff. Well rotted it will add life to your rhubarb and colour to your dahlias. It will make your grass grow lush and flavoursome. Not very well rotted and it will probably scorch the lot, it *is* powerful stuff.

All in all, growing grass can be a scientific progress from one biologically perfect blade of grass to the next. Or it can be like gardening on a large scale, a question of continual loving care. One important thing to remember about grass is that it grows on top of the soil. If you are aiming to have your soil in good heart, and at some stage to 'go arable', then there is no better protection for the soil than a good, clean crop of fertile grass.

FIELD CULTIVATION

In the effective use of land, the step up from producing foodstuffs on a horticultural scale is to consider cultivating whole fields with one crop. The most widely grown crop is grass which is harvested by man or beast and eventually becomes part of a food-producing chain. Producing food is what land use is about, although attention is sometimes given to the leisure aspect of land use or to the wildlife it supports. Mainly, however, we are concerned with supporting ourselves from the resources available and the basic resource is land. Having progressed from gathering what nature offered to specifically producing for our own consumption, mankind went through many different sagas of ingenuity to make his job easier. Ploughs were initially made of wood and in areas where wood was scarce, drift-wood was called into service. Although initially man pulled or pushed his own ploughs, some inspired and possibly exhausted human had the bright idea of harnessing animal power. If you ever try to plough a field using a highly bred hunter then you may get some idea of the exhilaration that must have accompanied those early trials. And, of course, the fury when the whole thing goes wrong and you wind up more exhausted than ever. However, man was clearly on the right track and animal ploughing progressed.

It was in 1767 that a Scottish gentleman, James Small from Berwickshire, had his invention, the chain plough, patented. This led to the development of the all-metal plough which remained in use until it in turn was superceded by the development of tractors and other related equipment. To cultivate land on anything other than the smallest scale you need a tractor or a team of horses. To handle and use horses on the land is a wonderful achievement; it is also a specialist occupation and if it is to pay its way the crops you produce must be high in value, or you should not be paying for the land you use, or you must be able to survive without earning very much. Anyone who can honestly deny all of those claims would be very welcome to contact us. We would love to be able to justify using horses on the land in an economic sense. Putting an income into your calculations from tourism or breeding draft-horses probably does put the whole venture into the black but that is beyond simply making money from cultivating.

Working Together

Having said then that a tractor is a necessity, the next decision is how large should it be. There is a vast range to choose from, starting at the humble grey Ferguson that was our first and certainly most loved tractor up to the vast monsters often seen ploughing in lines on the great expanses of Salisbury Plain. These monsters can cost you as much as a country cottage whereas the little Ferguson will cost you only a few hundred pounds. Of course, the little Ferguson will handle only light jobs, pulling trailers and light ploughing if you are lucky with your land. To do really heavy work you need a big machine although not a monster — something that costs around the same as a family saloon. You can still cultivate your acres without this capital expenditure if you employ a contractor. Many farmers use contractors on their land. The contractor covers thousands of acres a year and can justify the most up-to-date equipment. It is often more economic to employ such a contractor. Some are large companies, covering most of Britain; many are family-based organisations. The points to check are that the contractor has the sort of machinery you want used on your land and that the labour he employs will be capable of using it. Many contractor-farmer relationships are very happy. It is always worth asking around and getting a contractor who you know of at least by reputation. We once had a bit of ploughing done by a neighbour. We had omitted to check were he ploughed last and the result was a hitherto clean piece of land turning into a piece of land densely populated with docks. The labour required to remove the weed was far more than if we had ploughed the field ourselves. Finally, it is always worth checking that tractor tyres are washed off before they can contaminate your land.

Having decided how to cultivate your acres, you must consider what to grow. There is an interesting marketing difference between two sections of types of crop produced. Plant such crops as potatoes, cereals and sugar beet and you are concerned with National Boards or similar organisations who are basically marketing for you. You may well be involved in quotas and your aim will be to produce the correct amount of crop in the correct condition at the right time. Other crops such as peas and fruit are sold by private treaty and it is up to you to find a buyer at the right price at the time you require. Due to EEC pressures there are movements within the boards and organisations. This has only recently affected the hop market and we have yet to see how free competition within this area will alter the market. At the moment most hop farmers seem to think that business will carry on as usual but of course eventually the structure will alter. At one end of the scale of involvement, you can have all the work done on your land by contractor, grow a crop that is marketed for you and spend your life worrying that other people will not perform as well as you expect. At the other end of the scale, you can do things totally independently, choose crops with a free market, do all the cultivation yourself and spend all your life worrying that you yourself may not manage as well as you expect. Most people choose a middle course; we like to market our own produce but call in help when needed to produce it.

Man and Machine — Formidable Push Plough

To aid effective cultivation, many farmers follow a system of crop rotation. Rotation has been practised in Britain for hundreds of years. The aims of rotation are to keep the land as fertile as possible by deep manuring and cultivating a root crop using the humus and nitrogen build-up from grass seeds. Control of weeds is assisted by one year planting in the autumn, another in the spring and so on. This kind of alternate cultivation eradicates many stubborn weeds that would become a major problem if one crop were continuously grown. By alternating the types of plants grown, parasitic organisms are destroyed as their hosts are removed. Traditionally rotations were planned to spread labour requirements as effectively as possible throughout the year. An example of a six-year rotation is:

1. wheat;
2. roots;
3. cereal;
4. seeds (grass);
5. cereal — a different variety;
6. potatoes.

As grass seeds are expensive and modern plants perform well for several years, it is becoming common to run the seeds part of the rotation for two or three years. When this is intended, the seed mixture comprises several different grasses, clovers and other seeds. If the seeds are only for one year, then Italian ryegrass is often used as it is a heavy yielder. The benefit of rotation for a grazing animal lies in the fact that the life cycle of many of the parasites of animals is also broken. If the rotation is staggered around the farm then livestock can continually have clean grazing in front of them. This is an instance where the traditional idea of mixed farming shows its benefit to land and beast. Clearly a livestock enterprise based on permanent pasture has no such dramatic break and the land must be rested to lower the parasite population.

In the cereal break there are new factors influencing the choice of crop. Rye was for many years overlooked as a crop. However, with the growing interest in health foods there has been a boom in its demand. It is now one of the most profitable cereal crops to grow and deep ploughing apparently reduces the risk of ergot. (Ergot is a fungus that attacks rye which if consumed has an hallucinatory effect and is toxic.) When growing roots, they can either be harvested for sale or you can run sheep on them as winter fodder. The sheep eat the green and tread in the root and dung, adding manurial value to the soil. If you turn the roots up on to the surface the sheep will eat them too. Potatoes can be grown in the root break although they are in fact tubers. Today potatoes still seem to be the cheapest food on earth. Planting legumes to increase the nitrogen value in the soil is excellent if the following crop is to be wheat. It is disastrous if the next crop is malting barley as the barley will not be accepted due to its high nitrogen content. An interesting point about growing field beans is that the straw that remains after the beans have been threshed has an extremely high calorific value. This does not mean very much unless you choose to centrally heat your house using a multi-purpose burner. If your house is heated with such a device then you will probably decide to grow beans for ever. The straw is light to carry and heats magnificently. There is also quite a lot of general enthusiasm for a revival in growing beans to feed to livestock so the humble bean can fill your freezer with meat and heat your house.

Vegetables

A vast number of people grow vegetables. In country areas it has always been the rule rather than the exception and with the increase in enthusiasm for self-sufficiency in recent years, many more urban areas have followed suit. It is much cheaper to grow your own vegetables and they always taste far better than those bought in the shop. The trouble starts when your production outstrips demand. Even with a freezer there are times when you have to dispose of surplus crops. When the surplus has not been planned it is usually a case of passing out bunches of beans to friends and neighbours. Not many shops are interested in a spasmodic supply and the bulk does not justify the kind of packaging necessary to send the vegetables to market.

If you are green-fingered and have put some planning into your enterprise then it can be profitable. You have to decide at the start how you intend to make your enterprise work. You can either decide to produce a wide range of vegetables — as you would normally to feed your family, only on a larger scale. Or you can decide to produce large quantities of a few specific crops. If you feel your market is among people living locally who will come to you to buy their weekly vegetables, you should practise the former. If you do not wish or feel it is impracticable in your area to carry out a farm gate enterprise, choose the latter course. Clearly the amount you can produce is limited by the amount of land you have available and by the type of land. Early land, that is land in the south that naturally warms up early, can give you the advantage of reaching early maturity dates. A crop that is ready even two weeks before the majority reaps a good bonus. The lettuce is always a clear indicator of that. If you have lettuce ready for sale early and the weather is warm you can never keep up with demand. The price is good and with tremendous enthusiasm you raise more seed, encourage your seedlings. Then everybody else has their own little lettuce glut and you are faced with bolting lettuces and a price that has dropped to rock bottom. When the end of the season approaches, lettuce is again in high demand.

Showmanship — Country Style

It can often pay great dividends to wait a whole year before going into a vegetable enterprise. That way you can actually monitor the buying behaviour in your area and decide what to plant and which peaks to aim for. Either that or accept that there will be times when you cannot sell all you produce and vice versa. With bulk crops you must decide either to aim for the highest possible yield when the market is possibly at its lowest in cash terms or sacrifice quantity to try for an early market. There was a delightful example of enterprise a few years ago in Thanet, Kent. It is a great potato-growing area and vast acreages are planted. One farmer was unable to harvest a few acres of late potatoes as Winter set in early. He did not do the usual and plough them in. Instead, in the very early spring, he found that most of the potatoes were in excellent condition. So he harvested the lot, sorted them and sold them as the earliest new potatoes. It was a tale that has kept the farming community entertained for months — every year it is retold in the autumn and the spring. We have never tried it ourselves but like everyone else who hears it we say that we will one year.

SOIL

The initial requirement for producing vegetables is to have somewhere to grow them. Unless you are 'going hydroponic', that is aiming to grow plants in a solution of nutrients in water, you will need some land. When you walk on your land and dig around in it you can classify it. If the land is heavy, slow draining and impossible to dig in wet weather, you have to accept that your plants have a comparatively short growing season. You have to delay planting until Spring has warmed and dried the land. However, in high summer you do have an advantage in that your land holds the available water and is not so susceptible to drying out. If you can dig in large quantities of organic manure, some ash, sand, and carbonate of lime (except on alkaline soil), you will obtain heavy crops. Given this assistance, vegetables thrive on this soil. Choose suitable varieties for the heavy soil — for example, round-rooted carrots grow beautifully where long-rooted ones do not.

Chalk soils are produced where limestone is found below the top-soil. Often the top-soil layer is quite thin and the soil has a greyish look. Although very sticky in the rain, this soil dries quickly and you can work on it earlier than on heavy soil. Its advantage is that it very rarely requires liming where other soils do. Its disadvantage is that the soil can dry out very quickly and plants that suffer in drought never fully recover.

It is often worth mulching on clay soils to retain moisture. Applying large quantities of organic manure increases yields. If you grow broccoli and cabbages through the winter on this soil, they will need a dressing of a nitrogenous fertiliser or they will look miserable.

You should be happy if you have a well balanced mixture of clay and sand in your soil. Your soil is no doubt dark and friable, you can work happily on it for most of the year except directly after rain and your vegetable enterprise should flourish. Bearing in mind, of course, that all your neighbours have the same excellent soil, you will probably have to grow for a market some distance away and be involved in the packaging that involves.

With light, sandy soil you are able to plant very early in the spring. Every drop of water and fertiliser you add, however, is draining away at speed. It is therefore wise to delay the application of organic manure until after the main winter rains and also to apply any chemical fertilisers little and often. Even with generous mulching, you will probably need to irrigate in the summer. You can grow long, tapering carrots and parsnips and early cloche crops. Runner beans are happier in heavier soils so grow French beans instead. Farming vegetables in light soil seems more elegant than in heavy: the root vegetables are elegantly tapered and even the beans are French! And the soil does not walk around with you as our Kentish clay does. At the end of a wet day we walk around laden down with mud collars around our wellingtons. Our latest attempts to make our progress lighter has been to rub our boots with goose grease but unfortunately, this just makes the dogs wind in and out of legs trying to lick it off. The next attempt will have to be with something they do not like — perhaps diesel oil?

ORGANIC MANURE

If you are fortunate enough to have access to great quantities of this precious commodity, a great many of your problems are solved on any soil. If you have well rotted manure and straw mixed with animal droppings, ideally with a liberal mixture of poultry droppings for nitrogen, you can obtain heavy crops with little else added. Dried blood and bonemeal are also organic manures but are used in small quantities. Sewage sludge, although it sounds evil, is usually quite pleasant to handle. It is not available everywhere but where it is, it is often free or very inexpensive. There is a problem, however, as was proved on a local village cricket pitch. Lovingly maintained and fertilised, the green grass is the pride of the cricket club. One year it grew an excellent crop of tomatoes! Well, that is an exaggeration because the plants were not allowed to reach fruiting size. The sad truth is that treatment at the sewage plant does not destroy tomato seeds and under suitable conditions very hardy tomato plants will appear. We had a similar experience some years ago when our septic tank, hidden down at the end of a field, overflowed. A couple of months later the area of spillage was knee-deep in fruiting tomatoes. We leave you to guess whether we ate them or not! Deep litter poultry manure must be well rotted before use as it contains wood shavings. This usually pollutes the atmosphere so is not worth doing unless you have an area well away from neighbours and your own house. If you are intending to rely on garden compost to supply valuable organic material, become a waste miser and put absolutely everything you can on to it. Even a small amount of animal droppings, say from a pet rabbit, adds life to the compost heap. Certainly add household peelings and waste. Good leafmould takes a year to become suitable for application. The leaves should be layered with soil. There are often local speciality manures such as spent hops in brewing areas and wool shoddy near wool factories. The traditional methods of application of these substances are always the most efficient.

If you live near the sea, seaweed is really fantastic. You have to stack it for a month or so for most of the salt to be washed out. In fact, if it is gathered in a dry summer, you will have to water it. It really does produce heavy crops. If you feel tempted to bring some back from a holiday by the sea, it may be worth remembering that to be really effective you have to apply 12 lb per square yard. Even if your car will carry a hundredweight of it, you can only fertilise ten square yards, and of course you may well find your family refuses to appreciate the odour of decaying seaweed at close quarters. Preparations from a seaweed base for foliar application are available from garden centres. We often concoct our own liquid mixtures using well rotted manure and these are particularly effective if there is a dry spell and the plants are not able to draw all the required benefit from the soil. These liquid feeds are not a substitute for well-dug-in manure, just a helpful supplement. If you apply a general fertiliser to growing crops but do not dig it in, just sprinkle it on the ground — the rain will gradually water it in and it will reach all the roots instead of bypassing them.

CULTIVATION

You have now decided where and what to grow and the sort of manure you are going to use. If you are cultivating a new area, you may well have to remove grass. Before you dig it in or remove it and stack it somewhere to rot, it is worth considering whether you can sell it for turf. The best turf comes from new leys neatly cropped by sheep; your turf may be like this or it may be a portion of garden you are digging up with equally suitable lawn grass. In any case have a good look at it. There is nothing more heartening in a new venture than to get an instant cash return.

Whenever you are cultivating, remove and burn perennial weeds. Each weed you remove will save you dozens next year. Never be tempted to put such horrors on the compost heap or they will merrily return along with the manure. In fact, many permanent weeds grow from chopped up bits of themselves so you could greatly increase your problem if you hope to simply dig them in. Aim to have the area dug and manured by Christmas; you can then celebrate with an easy mind while frost and rain complete your work.

When you can get on to your land again depends on your soil type. Heavy soils mean late access; light soils mean you can get going early. In any case, you should now find that the top few inches of soil break down to a fine crumbly tilth when raked. You may find that the soil beneath is compacted. One cause of bad drainage is continually rotivating at a set depth: this causes the soil beneath to become compacted and water finds it difficult to drain away. If this is your problem, you will have to dig right down and loosen the bottom layer. This is remarkably heavy work and certainly worth avoiding by varying the heights at which you rotivate. If you have ditches near the area you are cultivating, keep them really clear. A well-cared-for ditch is a great help in draining land and one that is often overlooked on small land enterprises. By digging down an extra foot, ditches that have long ceased to be effective can be returned to active life. Watch an effective ditch at work when the weather is wet and imagine what all the water it is carrying away would do to the land it is draining. Without ditches it is more difficult to drain land. To drain a large area you may need to use land drains leading to a constructed soakaway. Envisaging all this digging may persuade you to practise small-scale ditch digging. This is really an application of polder farming. Dig ditches, with the lie of the land vertically down your plot, dig a ditch at the bottom leading to a collecting area such as a small pond. On clay soils you can construct a pond in a time-honoured way by using the natural clay as an impervious layer. If you live on different soil or do not have such faith in nature, you must resort to polythene liners. Of course, if you live on very light soil then you can run the whole system in reverse. Put the pond at the highest point and lead the ditches running away; if the soil is extremely light it is worth lining the ditches with polythene. These methods of carrying water to and from sources have been practised all over the world for centuries. It is amusing that now we have developed cheap plastic sheeting to make the whole process more foolproof, we seem to use the method less. This is, of course, partially due to a mechanised approach to vegetable production. When the enterprise is looked at from a smaller point of view, machine and daily labour requirements can take on a different position and it is often logical if you are producing on your own to use the winter months to construct waterways and drains so that the summer workload can be lessened.

When it comes to Summer and you are actually applying water to the vegetables, the essential point to remember is that when you water, do it enthusiastically. Lightly watered plants scorch in the sun, rain-watered plants do not, so that when water has to be applied artificially it must be in rain quantities, not in watering-cans. Water storage tanks are often necessary. In old garden systems they were often incorporated as part of a basic design. We have a greenhouse containing an enormous grapevine. It has its own tank that fills from the gutters and apparently from underwater drains. It has never gone dry and so there is always water on hand. Even a rain butt under a gutter collects a vast amount of rain in a downpour. Water storage puts two extra responsibilities on you. The first is to make sure that the water is completely safe from a child's point of view. Even if you do not have children, other people do and little children can trot remarkable distances when unguarded. A water tank is a potential killer and must be fenced in or covered. Your water storage can also be an ideal place for mosquitoes to breed and flourish. A drop of oil on the water surface cures that and in the summer it is well worth keeping an eye out for them. It is apparently only the females that bite but it is impossible for anyone but another mosquito to tell the difference, so do not bother with the niceties and kill the lot.

Designer Vegetable Growing: a small area like this — 60 ft deep, 30 ft wide — can be kept as a 'showpiece' while main crops grow on a field basis

One creature that anyone cultivating does not want to destroy is the earthworm. If you have applied generous quantities of manure, you will certainly increase this useful creature's numbers. The earthworm obligingly cultivates deep down into your soil by his continual ingesting and passing out of the soil. 'Baddies' in the vegetables such as slugs can be disposed of using proprietary killers or more profitably by letting egg-laying ducks do the work for you. The duck eats the slug (she loves the succulent beasts) and will give you eggs in return. Chickens love slugs too, but they will also eat your vegetables. Just a sprinkling of ducks keeps the ecological system working to your advantage. Instead of all that digging in the winter, you could let a few free-range pigs do a lot of the work for you. You can also use goats to eat their way deep into scrub and brambles. This all depends on whether you want to integrate different areas of production or not. Planning a kind of animal-assisted ideal life is very useful to fill in wet days when you cannot get on to the land. Of course, once you have committed yourself to the livestock you must be out irrespective of the weather. That is always a point worth remembering.

AFTER GERMINATION

When you look at the price of a packet of seeds you can instantly see the potential profit. A few pence produces pounds of crop. That is assuming that you are able to help the seeds along and also that the seeds are worth planting in the first place. There are always great differences in the price of seed on offer. The only real advice to follow is to choose seeds from a reputable company, buy them where you are sure they have been kept correctly and choose a suitable variety for your conditions. Last year we did not buy courgette seeds until the season was quite advanced. There were very few packets left in the shops and it was clearly too late to buy by mail order. We bought a brand that we had never heard of, the packets looked a little crumpled but the dates were still correct. The seedlings made a disappointingly sparse appearance and the plants had nothing like the vigour we had hoped for. Next year we shall order early; there is nothing more disappointing than labouring away at something that will never come up to standard.

If you are planning to plant a wide variety of standard crops, try to buy the seed by weight. There is not much point in going out and paying for dozens of pretty little packets when you are growing commercially. Seeds are usually tiny things (unless they are banana seeds), but they need warmth anyway. Do not be tempted into sowing too thickly: it makes thinning unnecessarily time-consuming and is wasteful. There are all sorts of tips on how to plant small seeds. You can mix them with sand and sprinkle the lot along a row, you can sprout the seeds in wallpaper paste and put that into an icing bag and dribble it along the row. If you have a steady hand, you can simply deal with them by hand.

When producing crops for sale you must find the balance between over-effort and under-effort. To produce single specimen parsnips is an enviable achievement unless you intend to make money selling them. Rather produce a larger quantity of good parsnips and leave out the 'stars'. All growing is like that if done to be commercial. Your product has to be excellent to sell but not so excellent that it becomes uneconomical to produce it. That is why it is worth getting a head start by having the ground well manured and buying good seeds. When the growing and harvesting season is under way you will need all the time available to keep up with gathering and packing without having to encourage undernourished plants or pamper 'prima donnas'.

Weeding becomes a pressing occupation during the growing season. After all the ideal growth area that you have prepared for your vegetables is also a paradise for weeds. Using weedkillers can today cut down a vast amount of labour. However, weedkillers are of necessity very powerful toxic substances. We use as few of these substances as we can, partly because we do not like putting chemicals near the food we intend to sell or eat and partly because we do not like having dangerous substances around. Anything of this nature should be kept in a locked cupboard.

We grow a lot of our crops in blocks rather than in traditional rows. This increases ground cover and if you keep the weeds at bay in the early stages the plants soon become big enough to make their own way. Planting closer together than usual also helps this method. It means that things like beetroot and lettuces tend to be harvested while they are smaller than most for sale. This achieves two objects: first, it decreases the amount of possible damage from slugs and other things that eat into your growing plants and secondly, it provides a more attractive crop. A bunch of beetroot, the globes some 1½ to 2 inches across, tied with raffia around the stalks with the deep green leaves still attached, is a beautiful sight. Buyers at the farm gate and local shops will often be tempted by this natural presentation to buy. Once the beetroot grow to a standard three or more inches in diameter, your product is just the same as that available everywhere. You have lost the advantage that smaller scale production can have.

If you aim to encourage the public to buy directly from you, plan the vegetable area with visual effect in mind. Marrows are quite spectacular in growth. Plant them in a compost heap and the trailing variety will soon cover the area with umbrella leaves and bright yellow flowers. The flowers themselves can be harvested and stuffed and deep-fried. Perhaps your customers are not aware of this — a small recipe sheet often inspires specialist buying. There are some examples of ones that we have successfully used in Chapter 17. Leave some of the yellow flowers to grow into marrows and you have had two incomes from one crop. Selling on a farm gate scale means that you can also bundle together succulent little carrots taken as thinnings from a main carrot crop. These little carrots do not look beautiful for long as they wilt in a dry atmosphere but if they are sold quickly and cooked gently, they are the most delicious carrots of all. Everyone, public and shopkeeper alike, will be encouraged to buy if you can chat about the special delights of your products. Become an enthusiastic vegetable-eater and the feeling will soon come across to other people. When you see what a small portion of housekeeping fresh vegetables have become, it proves that there is scope for an enthusiast. Some health shops will sell fresh vegetables — they must usually be organically grown. Many young housewives have been brought up almost entirely on a diet of frozen vegetables. The same customers are often the ones with a keen interest in cooking so if you can put a tempting array of vegetables in front of them, you will have willing buyers. A trip to the continent always shows what many of us are missing: there every little corner grocery seems to offer a tempting variety of fresh vegetables. You can even carry the presentation theme as far as preparing strings of onions for sale. It is quite simple, you simply tie the dried onion stalks to a piece of string and form a chain. While we would not think of suggesting that the vegetable growers of Britain take to their bikes as the French used to do to sell us their onions, it is certainly a product with tremendous visual and culinary appeal.

SPECIALIST VEGETABLES

There are a few seedsmen who now specialise in selling exotic varieties of vegetable seeds. In a suburban area, the market for exotic vegetables like yellow tomatoes and red beans can often be tapped through a high-class greengrocer's or health shop. There are often even outlets in supermarkets in towns.

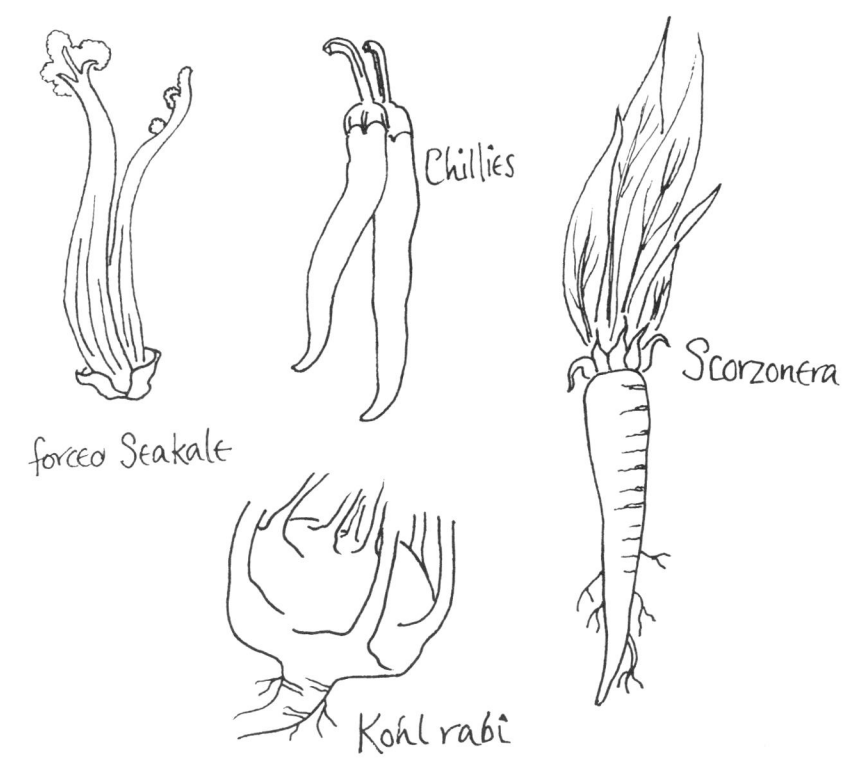

Some Exotic Vegetables

The essentials for exotic vegetables are professional packaging and standard production. It is much more complicated to produce a succession of exotic vegetables through the season than to grow the traditional crops. However, if that kind of challenge appeals to you, it is certainly most worthwhile and often a lot of fun. Children, and adults who have never come across tiny cherry tomatoes, are hooked for life. How about growing spaghetti plants? Even a few regular customers becoming converted to the fascination of eating hitherto unseen varieties leads to continuing sales. Even vegetables that were once popular, such as sea-kale, are unknown by many today. Often all a vegetable like this needs to increase its local popularity is a recipe leaflet. If you consider how we all happily consume avocado pears, kiwi fruits and other exotic fruits it is clear how powerful effective marketing is.

Some less usual vegetables to consider are Jerusalem artichokes. Grow the smooth-skinned variety; their long stalks make excellent game cover. Globe artichokes are delicious but never as prolific here as on the continent. Asparagus peas are tiny tender little things and very popular in a speciality market. Try unusual coloured beans and even home-grown haricot beans. Haricot beans do not provide a heavy crop but they are finer in flavour than the mass-produced ones. If you follow a really good, complicated recipe for baking them, guess what? They taste just like canned ones! Not nearly as many red beetroot are sold fresh as cooked but there are a lot of good recipes for borsch about and if you introduce them to your customers, you can sell the fresh roots. To sell Brussels sprouts pull up the whole plant. Hung upside down in a shed, the sprouts stay fresh for a few weeks. This often encourages people to try fresh as opposed to frozen ones. Red cabbage is delicious cooked or uncooked; it sells well in areas with a continental population.

Cardoons are appreciated on the continent but you will have to do some customer-education here with a recipe leaflet. They look rather like globe artichokes but it is not the spiky globes that you are after. Tie black polythene around the plant in mid-September to blanch the stems: this is the part you cook, using the same recipes you would use for celery. Celeriac is now sold in many supermarkets. It is a celery-flavoured root and really at its best fresh. Chicory is interesting to grow; you produce a root from seed, then you dig it up and force it in pots in the dark and up come those shiny nobs of chicory (some varieties produce a pink chicon). Corn Salad looks like forget-me-nots. You can eat it in the winter when other salad stuff is in short supply and it makes an excellent salad mixed with thinly sliced red cabbage and a few nuts. Courgettes are not really very special unless you grow yellow ones. If you live near an area with a continental population, grow a few big dandelions and blanch them; these are delicious in salads and much appreciated by healthy eaters because of their beneficial effect on the liver. Endive is another salad vegetable not appreciated so much here as it is on the continent. It has a bitter flavour and we only like it when it is mixed with lettuce.

Egg-plants (aubergines) grow remarkably well if they are well manured. We have tried egg-plants under glass and out in the garden and found that they preferred a sheltered spot in the garden where they grew enthusiastically. They look very decorative and like being used as patio plants in pots as long as the bottom half of the pot is filled with rotted manure. Fennel is another decorative vegetable to grow and its aniseed flavour is very refreshing. Garlic grows well in good soil but not to the enormous size of Italian bulbs unless you use a giant variety. Usually we grow ours from healthy garlic cloves bought wholesale. There is a variety of giant bulb on sale from one of the specialist seedsmen and we are going to try it this year — apparently it has a mild flavour. If you edge your vegetable area with nasturtium, you can pick the seed heads and pickle them like capers. Shallots are worth growing because they are often not available from ordinary greengrocers and are necessary in many recipes. Peppers grow well, especially under polythene tunnels. If you pick some of them while they are still small, it gives the keen cook a chance to preserve them in oil and vinegar. Salad potatoes have a waxy flesh and make the most delicious potato salad; they also sell for a lot more money than ordinary potatoes. Growing several varieties of radish offers your purchaser a wider variety; French Breakfast are our favourite ones. Winter radishes are cooked in the same way as turnips.

The farmer's name for kale is fodder but for humans it provides greenery at a time of year when hardly anything else is available. Salsify and scorzoneras are similar in appearance, both being long tapering roots with a green growth on top. The main difference between them is that salsify is a brown-skinned root and scorzoneras have a black skin. They have different flavours but are cooked in the same way. You can eat the leaves chopped in a salad; the roots should be cooked in acidulated water and are delicious in cream sauces or deep-fried. They grow rather like carrots and as they are hardy, you can leave them in the ground until you wish to lift them. Sea-kale, like asparagus, requires a permanent bed; as with chicory, you grow the root in the ground, lift it and then force succulent young shoots to grow. You can eat the unforced green leaves, using them as you would spinach; the blanched stems should be boiled in acidulated water and served with butter or a sauce. All the different types of spinach are worth growing; you can have some of at least one variety available all year and good-looking fresh spinach sells well. Pumpkins are great fun to grow and very decorative — they always look like great big plastic monsters lurking in the vegetables and there seems to be a returning enthusiasm for using them at Halloween. This year we saw a lot imported from Spain and they were astonishingly expensive, compared to the price fetched by a similar vegetable, the marrow. There are other exotic squashes and continentals and Americans certainly use them far more than we do. All the odd-shaped tomatoes are worth growing for a specialist market, in particular the really giant ones: they were fetching twice the price of their humbler cousins this summer.

Well, that is a list of the more unusual vegetables. No doubt we have left many out. Add to them all the standard vegetables, like carrots and onions, and it goes to show what an enormous choice we could have available in Britain.

Remember, any kind of root vegetable has a very limited life if you wash it to improve its appearance. Interestingly enough if you wash it you are theoretically carrying on a different business from simply growing and selling produce and could require a change of use planning permission. Farm gate sales of home-grown vegetables and fruit often leads on to other things and many smallholders happily sell oranges and plastic-wrapped cucumbers that clearly were never grown on site. In an area where planning officials are plentiful this can lead to conflict.

Soft Fruit Growing

Growing soft fruit is a traditional country occupation that has spread to suburban gardens and town allotments. Strawberries, raspberries and currants all taste of Summer and part of the joy of picking and stalking these fruits is the delicious juice that stains. Convert the fruit into jams and jellies and you have captured the flavour of Summer for the winter. Making preserves is another traditional country pursuit that has gone into urban kitchens. You can grow the fruit on an allotment, take it home and make jam that is quite indistinguishable from that made by the country dweller who simply walks up the garden. If you do not have plants that are already established and growing, you have one of two choices: you can either plant from scratch or you can bypass that bit and buy the fruit from a local market. Either way the aim is to put the finest available fruit into the preserving pan. Fine jelly is made from fine fruit. When you are picking the fruit it is always worth picking at the peak of perfection: there is no point in letting the plant work on to produce overripe fruit — that energy is put to better use producing another berry.

RASPBERRIES

If you are fortunate enough to live in Scotland, you may well be able to pick these delicious fruits growing wild. These wild berries have more flavour than the bigger, cultivated ones. However, if you do not live near such a delicious wild crop or would rather not trust that your competitors will not get there first, you must grow your own. Raspberries need good drainage but prefer heavy soils in which to grow. They thrive on well rotted manure so put a good layer in the bottom of the trench in early autumn. It must be well rotted; many manures, especially pig manure, will scorch and kill roots if the manure is not sufficiently aged. The best time to plant the canes is in early Winter. If you have to leave it until the spring, the canes will need special coddling should the summer be a dry one.

Make sure that the canes are from a virus-free crop. Raspberries are especially susceptible to virus attack. Whole varieties have been wiped out by these attacks. Ask your supplier for a Ministry of Agriculture certificate to prove that the stocks are certified. The canes should be one year old. If your site is well prepared and free from perennial weeds, the canes should establish themselves well and quickly. Cut the canes down to one foot in height in February. In May apply some good compost or well rotted manure all over the rows to a depth of one or two inches. Raspberries like being mulched as their roots are fibrous and shallow — they rarely reach down more than six inches. You can erect a trellis-type arrangement on to which the growing canes can be tied. Or you can put wires stretched horizontally either side of the canes: with this arrangement you do not have to tie the canes in as they lean on the wires.

It is possible to be picking raspberries through into the autumn if you plant some autumn-fruiting varieties. In any case, whenever the fruits are ready the birds will be waiting. Birds seem to have a never-failing appetite for raspberries. Sometimes they strip the whole berry and at other times they simply steal one side, leaving odd-shaped half berries all over the canes. You can either put up a cage that you can walk into to pick or you can drape the canes with net that you lift up when you are gathering. The most decorative and romantic rows of raspberries are those covered with old net curtains. The cream net floats on soft breezes, the deep reds and greens gleaming through. Funnily enough this kind of net is much easier to deal with than the specialist nets made for the job. The very fine net does not allow pieces of leaf and cane to poke through and catch the net. However, if you stick to the net curtains you may well be limiting the size of your rows — horticultural net is much cheaper to buy.

Whether you aim to sell the fruit fresh or to process it, you should aim to pick and dispose of it very quickly. Raspberries do not keep at all well when fresh. Put into little plastic punnets for resale, the bottom layers immediately start to produce juice and within hours can go mouldy. The best answer is to pick early in the morning and to deliver them first thing to the retailer, giving him all day to sell the punnets. It is when they have to stay overnight that problems really set in. 'Pick your own' is a very established way of selling soft fruit. The advantages are that you do not have to pay and look after the labour picking your fruit; the disadvantages are that the public is often unaware of the damage that children and careless adults can do to a crop. Also if you employ the labour, you can specify that all the ripe fruit on a cane must be picked; casual picking leaves ripe fruit to go mouldy and contaminate others. If you do allow 'pick your own', then you must check that the plants are being kept in good shape at the end of the day. If you limit the access to a few rows rather than the whole crop you will get better picking, but no-one wants to feel that they are having to struggle to find enough, so you have to strike a natural balance.

STRAWBERRIES

Summer would not be Summer without strawberries and cream. You can choose from giant, fist-sized berries down to the tiny Alpine strawberry. Strawberries can grow in herbaceous borders or in special beds — their low ground covering habit can make them suitable in a low-maintenance garden — and the trailing varieties look stunning on patios and terraces. You can grow them in tall, hollow pillars — cascades of green with succulent red fruits. With plenty of manure, the obliging fruit produces pounds of berries from a single plant. We grow Alpine strawberries as path edgings. One Alpine strawberry, then a lemon balm plant and so on. (The smell of lemon in the evening is beautiful and as it is a herb, it is also a crop.) The Alpine strawberries produce right through the summer and in sheltered spots you can even find the odd berry in winter. Like raspberries, the strawberry is a favourite with the birds, although at least some of the fruits are hidden under the spreading leaves.

Layering Strawberries

To start a strawberry bed, dig in plenty of manure. All these soft fruits require food and water to perform to their best ability. Strawberries usually increase by runners. Runners are the little plants that they send out which root into the ground and start to grow on their own. As strawberries are naturally woodland plants, you can make them feel really at home by applying plenty of leafmould. If you can plant the new plants in August, you will get an excellent crop next year. When your plants have flowered, apply straw or polythene as a mulch. This keeps the fruit off the ground. Netting will keep the birds off. If you decide to grow Alpine strawberries, the simplest way is to buy them from a nurseryman as little plants. However, seeds planted in March will fruit the same year and they are clearly much cheaper. By selecting different varieties, you can pick strawberries well into the autumn. If you are selling the fruit into the retail trade, make sure that the berries are quite dry before putting them into punnets. Wet fruit rots quickly. We live in a strawberry-producing area and the shops are empty after a shower of rain.

Strawberry jam is traditional with scones and cream. It is delicious if well made and always sells well. When you work out the costings on producing jam from your strawberries, make sure that you are not turning your produce into jam when you would obtain a far higher price for the strawberries by selling them direct.

If your strawberries are ready before or after the general crop, you will receive a considerable boost in retail price.

BLACKCURRANTS

These are the highest yielders of Vitamin C among home-grown fruits. Many acres of blackcurrants are sold on contract to the producers of blackcurrant drinks. Blackcurrant jam must be well made or the currants are tough. It has been used traditionally to soothe sore throats and as a cold remedy. It does not sell in anything like the quantity of strawberry or raspberry jam. The fresh fruit does not sell in such quantity either through retail outlets. In fact, it is often not stocked very widely when in season and it may well be worth advertising to bring in custom. There are new varieties that look like large blackcurrants available now. They taste of very little when eaten raw but when made into jam, they taste of blackcurrants. It is worth checking with the supplier of your plants what the varieties you are considering were bred for: these new varieties, which are heavy-yielding plants, would be ideal if you are intending to make jam but they would not bring a repeat order from a customer who eats them raw.

There are two major enemies of blackcurrants: big bud mite and reversion. If your plants do not fall prey to these, they may well fruit on happily for some thirty years. Plant new bushes during the winter, as early as possible. A mulch applied around them in May will protect the roots which are very near to the surface. They dislike being weeded. Blackcurrants are produced on wood that grew the previous year so pruning must aim to cut out as much old wood as possible and to keep the required wood in a reasonable shape for harvesting. Many rows of blackcurrants are now harvested by machine. It has become popular to encourage a 'pick your own' trade to clear the bushes after the machines have passed as they often miss branches and sometimes whole plants. This kind of 'pick your own' will probably have a limited life as very few customers enjoy walking along endless clear rows to find the occasional loaded bush.

There is obviously more interest in picking fruits such as strawberries and raspberries that can be instantly consumed. However, often the clients for 'pick your own' currants are more knowledgeable than those who pick their own strawberries and raspberries. As the pickers may well appreciate what they are doing, it is worth considering 'pick your own' for currants even if you decide against it for the other fruits because of possible damage.

REDCURRANTS

For these fruits and for yellow and white currants, the aim in pruning is not the same as when working on blackcurrants because these currants fruit on old wood. You can grow them as bushes or even train them against a wall or fence as a cordon. They are best planted in November. Cover the surrounding soil with straw — up to one foot deep — directly after planting. The shape to aim for when pruning is an open goblet. Birds are even more cunning with their consumption of these currants. They actually consume the flower buds if allowed to. Tying black thread between the branches helps or the bushes can be put into a fruit cage. When the fruit is ready, pick the whole sprig. Although the market for these currants is rather more specialist, it is there. Certainly if you make redcurrant jelly, it will sell very well in the weeks approaching Christmas. If the fruits are for retail sale, then as long as they are dry when picked they will keep fairly well.

If you are intending to make jam from any of the currant family, you will be faced with the time-consuming chore of removing the currants from their strigs. Freeze them, put them into a tin and shake furiously. The stalks and currants will separate, making the job much easier. There is no difference in the jam you make. If you freeze the currants on open trays they take hardly any time at all. Of course, if you are intending to make jelly then you can leave the currants on their strigs — it will not make any difference to the final result. Usually we put the remainder of currants left after straining them to make jelly into apple chutney. For this we have to go back to strigging the currants.

GOOSEBERRIES

These are the first of the soft fruits mentioned that actually fight back when you pick them. The other fruits may well leave stained fingers as proof of consumption but the humble gooseberry actually inflicts wounds. It is worth bearing in mind from the outset that if the plant is encouraged to grow openly you will have a much easier task at harvest. As mildew is a problem in low-growing bushes, select ones that are growing on a short piece of trunk. Plant it so that the stem is above the ground. Gooseberries like being planted in November but will survive if planted with care any time up until February. Cover the surrounding soil with straw to a depth of one foot in May. The first berries will appear around Whitsun. If you pick the biggest of the berries then the other ones will have more room to grow and receive more nourishment. With really large dessert varieties, the berries must be allowed plenty of room. The most delicious of all the gooseberries are the giant deep red ones, just at the point of bursting with sweet juice. Gooseberry jam for some reason is rarely a fast seller. Although it is quite delicious as is gooseberry curd, this like all the curds does not keep well and can only really be sold to delicatessens, smothered in 'sell by' dates. The aggravation is probably not worth it. Making for your own consumption certainly is. It can, of course, make your reputation if you are selling cream teas. A plate of fresh scones, a bowl of home-made clotted cream and small pots of lemon, orange and gooseberry curd — Mmmmmm. Taking the gooseberry into catering for lunches or buffets leads to gooseberry pies, gooseberry sauce with fresh mackerel and possibly glazing the top of small round raised pies with a thin layer of bright green gooseberry jelly.

BLACKBERRIES

These are another fruit that can fight back. With some varieties the thorns are bred out, but somehow some of the flavour seems to be lost, too. Blackberries are excellent to grow up fences and walls. Even one plant will produce excellent fruit as blackberries are self-fertile. They are best planted in November but can take being moved as late as March. Cut the plant down to nine inches above the ground and arrange whatever form of support you prefer.

You can train pairs of fruit to grow over trellis over a garden path. The thornless varieties are certainly worth considering for this type of location. You can, of course, use the thorns to your advantage by planting them to cut off a route for marauding cats or similar nuisances. Blackberries are very attractive plants to watch growing. They always seem to have first flowers, then tiny green berries, followed by larger green berries and then varying sizes of black ones — this progression starts in late August and goes through well into October. This obliging plant will happily produce more of itself if you poke the end of a growing shoot into the ground. Do this in late summer and by November you can sever the new plant from its parent and move it. The biggest berries can be sold as dessert fruit. The rest of the crop can be processed into jams, pies, chutneys and wines. You can even dry the young leaves of the blackberry to make a sort of tea.

Gooseberries — early fruit thinnings make excellent pies. Use later, heavy, crop for processing.

BLUEBERRIES

To be quite different, why not grow this great American favourite? The plants are in fact related to our native blueberry and, like their wild ancestor, like a peaty soil. As they are very ornamental, they can be grown in a herbaceous border or as part of a decorative plan in the soft fruit area. Dig plenty of peat into the ground before planting and — for once — do not apply manure. Blueberries fruit on the tip of the last season's growth so the aim in pruning is to remove old stems and encourage the fruiting ones. They are quite hardy and disease-free. Apply a general fertiliser in March and when harvest-time comes, be prepared to go repeatedly over the bush removing fruit as it ripens. As there are few blueberries cultivated in Britain, you may find the simplest market is to put them into punnets and sell them to retailers. They also make excellent jam and as our American cousins claim, excellent pies. They go extremely well with cheesecake.

*The Highly Ornamental Blueberry,
Cousin of the Wild Bilberry*

The Flower Garden and the Herb Garden

THE FLOWER GARDEN

Anyone with a garden probably grows at least a few flowers. To grow flowers for sale can be very simple indeed. You can advance round an established garden, scissors in hand and snip off attractive bunches during most of the summer months. In some locations, such as country cottage doorsteps, these are the bunches that will probably sell best. With a nice mixture of colours and shapes and a generous bunch for the price, such bunches do not last very long on a good weekend.

If you decide to grow specifically, the choice of flowers depends on your location and how you intend to sell the flowers. With no passing market you will have to sell to greengrocers, florists or hotels and restaurants for display. Almost all of these markets will require standard-looking flowers. Unless you are growing on a large scale, it is probably not worth considering growing under glass. Flowers grown this way are necessarily more expensive; even if you are not heating the greenhouse you are at least having to maintain it. To consider growing flowers in a heated greenhouse you must feel very sure indeed of your market. There is a great deal of competition in selling these kinds of flowers, including a lot of imported flowers. Cut flowers have a short life and they do not have a long time to sell on the shop shelf. Good strong growers, such as dahlias grown on a well manured plot, have an attractiveness all their own. So do well grown chrysanthemums and, going to the other extreme, delicate sweet peas. As with other growing enterprises, it is worth aiming to catch the early or late markets. To grow the earliest sweet peas you can use cloches; you can slow the growth of chrysanthemums by leaving the pots out until the very last moment. All these flowers must be presented to the consumer in top condition. This is also the case with pot plants. Although it may seem that a pot plant will happily survive far longer than cut flowers, this is not the case unless you alone are looking after them. A pot plant dislikes being overwatered more than it does being underwatered. If the plant you carefully raised from seed is left to the tender mercies of several different shop assistants then both will happen to the unsuspecting creature and it will die. Many outlets for flowers, cut and potted, will insist on sale or return. If the flowers die then so does your profit. Some garages and hotels will enter into arrangements for you to keep them continually supplied with flower arrangements. Again willing hands will overwater and careless hands will deposit cigarette ends on plants. It is not a case of do not do the business. It is a case of being fully prepared for what will happen to plants out of your control.

The public is being artificially educated to demand only a very small range of plants. Look at the highly professional displays of flowers and plants for sale in the high street and in markets: the range available is continually decreasing. It is often possible to use this aspect of the market to your advantage. Become established in the area in which you live as a specialist producer. If the public know that you can supply quite beautiful blooms at competitive prices, you will start to build an enterprise. People buy flowers for occasions — weddings and funerals — and for regular events. When we produced chrysanthemums regularly, we had a customer on the last week in October every year. It was for a bunch of one dozen of the finest blooms to take to a crematorium. Off they went like clockwork every year to commemorate our customer's mother. When our aged greenhouse gave way under a heavy fall of snow, we gave up as we felt that a new large greenhouse would not justify itself. It was hard to tell who felt the most upset that October, us or our customer. We still miss the big blooms and no doubt she would still have been turning up to buy them. That is the kind of trade that is not dependent on impulse-buying and is not adversely affected by highly commercial competition in the high street.

An area that is always of interest in the winter is dried flowers.

48 / THE FLOWER GARDEN AND THE HERB GARDEN

Victorian Floral Vocabulary

Fuchsia – Confiding love

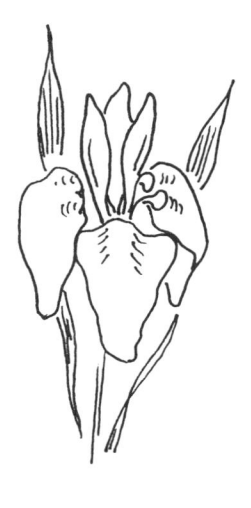

Iris – a message for you

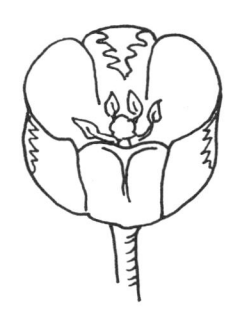

Tulip – declaration of love

Geranium – Friendship

Today there is a strong sale in silk flowers and other similar items that decorate without dying as fresh flowers do. There are a wide variety of flowers that can be grown specifically for drying. Everlasting flowers — the pink, yellow and blue tiny flower heads carried on spriggy branches — are popular in rural areas. Where a more sophisticated flower is demanded, there are still ideal subjects to be found in rural gardens. The pearl-sheened seed heads of dried Honesty mixed with orange dried Chinese Lanterns make an elegant arrangement. Many hydrangeas dry well; we have one that if picked late in the year dries to a soft green. This unusual colour looks fresh all winter. Try adding some choice: the hazel catkins available in January and possibly some peacock feathers (you can buy these from stately homes sometimes). A fabulous addition to a dried flower selection is provided by dried hops. If you can get them on long swags and gently dry them, you can offer them to restaurants and hotels as large pieces of decoration; cut into smaller pieces, they make delightful centrepieces for a table. Hops are brittle when dry and will crush if handled harshly. If that happens to your hops turn them into a hop pillow for sale or, if you are really desperate, turn them into beer! By producing a range of dried flowers that is not already widely available through florists, you can attract business that may well have been lost in the past due to the standardisation of many of the dried plants on offer. Dried flowers can be processed further to make framed pictures and cards. If you are really proficient at drying flowers, it may be worth advertising that you will preserve wedding bouquets. Just a few flowers from the bouquet can be dried, arranged into a framed picture and the bride has a permanent reminder.

THE HERB GARDEN

A garden of herbs can consist of just a few plants to satisfy the culinary needs of the family or it can grow to immense proportions to provide fresh and dried herbs for sale for culinary and health purposes. There is a great deal of interest in the use of herbs in medicine. Even if this does not involve combining herb essences and concoctions, it can be taken as simply as chopped herbs in a mixed salad that have a restorative effect. The herbs can be grown to be sold in little fresh bunches or they can be dried before sale. They can be sold growing in pots or put into sachets for discouraging moths, or pillows to gently aid sleep. These final herb products often end up being made in a workshop or indoors. The growing of herbs is an outdoor occupation. You can put the entire venture into one annual package: tending the plants as they come to maturity, gathering and picking at the right times, drying as you go. Then in the winter months when the outside work slackens off, you can go inside to produce the herb sachets.

There are various factors to consider before planting a herb garden. To produce a bulk crop of herbs, it may seem easiest to grow the plants in rows as a normal crop. But if you intend to have customers coming to you, this less than romantic approach may well lower their enthusiasm. Appearance is often important in this market. By working out on a piece of graph paper the heights and colourings of various herbs it is possible to produce a garden-like setting in a field environment. A good way to start this effect is to plant a new lawn — a chamomile lawn. Raise some plants from seed and plant them in April. The plants need four inches between them. In the first season let the plants flower freely; from then on mow the lawn with the blades at the highest cut. Walking on this lawn releases a gentle perfume. Chamomile tea made from the dried flowers is good for insomnia and makes a hair rinse for fair hair. There is a good market for nicely packaged herb teas. Dried mint makes another excellent tea as does dried marigold. Marigolds are another attractive herb to grow. Sage, rosemary, thyme and lavender are permanent plants. Established as a thick border, they give a herb area a feeling of permanence. You can make the internal layout complicated as in an Elizabethan knot garden or plan it on simpler modern lines. A central raised area could be planted with an exotic-looking herb such as bergamot. This is sometimes referred to as bee balm and if you choose a variety with red flowers, it is a striking plant.

Dill is delicious with fish; angelica can be candied. Nasturtium seeds can be pickled like capers and lavender dried to make lavender sachets for perfuming drawers and cupboards. Balm has a distinctive lemon flavour — we use it in yoghurt or chopped in salads. Herbalists prescribe its use for gastric disorders and migraine. With such a wide variety to choose from, many purchasers are using herbs widely rather than specifically. Continual use of a quantity of herbs in your diet is a form of preventative medicine. (Of course, it is important not to make too many claims for the herbs you produce. Although some people use them as a total alternative to modern medicine, such treatment could be dangerous.) Bay leaves have been used to treat anorexia: perhaps a clue to this lies in the fact that the flavour of bay subtly enhances the flavour of food without being overpowering. Comfrey is grown in great quantities by some believers. You can revert to Tudor ideals and make bone-healing compresses from an infusion of the leaves. Comfrey can also be used for congestion: the roots and leaves should be well boiled and the cooking water reduced before consumption. The old names for this apparently boundless plant were knit bone and boneset. Apart from all this, comfrey leaves make excellent compost and they are produced in abundance if the plants are cropped three times a year. You can also force the young growths to eat like asparagus.

A Selection of Herbs

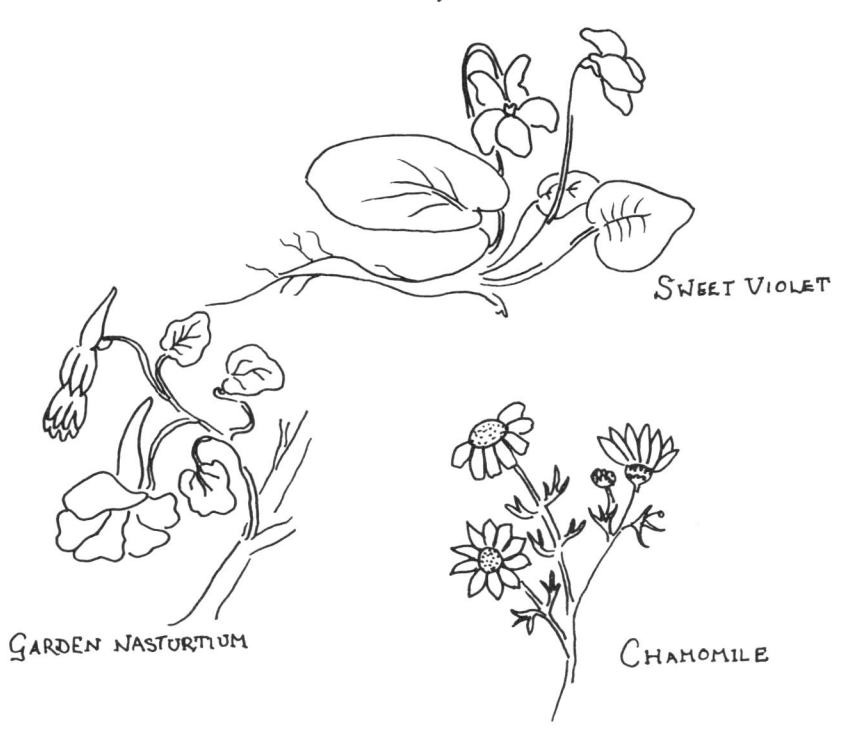

SWEET VIOLET

GARDEN NASTURTIUM

CHAMOMILE

One of the delights of becoming involved with growing and selling herbs is that you begin to amass a great amount of lore from your customers. Hyssop tea is a great standby for winter coughs and colds in many families. Dill water soothes babies; parsley helps with inflammation of the kidneys. The delicate English violet can produce a liquid for soothing catarrhal infections. (Alternatively, put the violet fresh into salads.)

For an effective salve, heat a handful of marigold petals in some Vaseline jelly, warm and strain it. The resulting salve is soft and soothing for the skin. Mix in a spoonful of clear honey and the moisture-retaining ability of the treated skin is improved. Using various herbs, salves with special applications can be produced. They should never be designed to provide quick, harsh treatment; the accent of all these kinds of product is to gently soothe.

A mixture of herbs in a muslin bag dropped into a warm bath not only perfumes the bather: the bath can also have a soothing effect if the herb mixture contains natural sedatives such as lime blossom. If you put in rosemary and lavender, the bath is stimulating. We always put a quantity of natural sea salt into these bath bags and gently bruise the dried herbs to allow them to release their oils. We sell herb bags prettily packaged with ribbons and coloured labels. They are not expensive items and are popular as gifts in the summer and at Christmas.

Pot pourri, which is a mixture of flower heads and leaves preserved with some of their essential oils, is always popular. Along with herbs like lavender and rosemary, sweet rose petals and geranium leaves go into the pot pourri. You can either buy mixtures of the oils and spices you need or you can make up your own. You will need four heaped tablespoons of orris root, one tablespoon each of cloves, ground nutmeg and allspice. Mix this up with the juice and rind of three lemons and stir in half an ounce of oil of bergamot. This mixture should go into a large pot. As you gather flowers to go into the pot pourri, mix handfuls of them with pinches of salt and saltpetre and leave them to dry for a few hours in the sun. Then put the dried petals into the big bowl, stir and cover. Keep doing this until the pot is full. At the end of the summer the pot pourri will be ready. You can concoct many different mixtures based on different flowers and each will be a perfumed reminder of Summer through the winter.

Herb Sachets

Bouquet garnis can be made using tiny muslin squares. Put into a cellophane outer bag and prettily labelled, they are popular in specialist groceries and as gift items. Thyme, bay, parsley and tarragon are traditional in these little bags. Put the little twig bundles on to the muslin square and tie the muslin to make a little bag. You can experiment with other mixtures. Special ones for cooking game are very nice. We add bought juniper berries to home-grown thyme and dried balm: this is delicious with wild duck. Using the little muslin bags means that you can put in whole spices and slivers of dried orange peel that would be unpleasant whole in a casserole. Much of the selling of herbs lies in giving information and making suggestions. A lot of nice products such as the bags for smelling drawers really sell because of their pretty packaging. Even herbs growing in pots sell better if the pots are slightly unusual, such as hand-thrown ones. If the thought of growing all these personable plants appeals to you but the thought of pretty packaging does not then it is a good area for a joint venture. There is bound to be someone who would enjoy doing the fiddly tying of muslin bags and the designing of colourful labels who would hate to be involved with growing the initial product.

The Orchard and the Vineyard

Nothing can be more pleasant on a warm summer's day than to be able to sit in a fine orchard, a hive of bees gently murmuring in the distance, a few sheep contentedly cropping the short grass. In the dappled light you can daydream of all the things you intend to be busily doing — next year. In sad reality in most of the orchards today you may well be run over if not asphyxiated by a rampant crop-spraying tractor. Producing apples and pears for sale can be a frustrating experience. Despite continual movements by our own apple-growers the continental varieties fill our shops. Their uniformity of size and colour means that the customer knows exactly what he is purchasing and, of course, the advertising that backs up the product is superb. Many different varieties are being produced to compete and large sums of money are being spent by brave growers on the presentation of their products. All this really seems to show is that anyone thinking about trying to make money from apples and pears either needs great capital resources or needs their head examining.

But it need not be either of these. To start planting vast orchards is certainly a nerve-racking venture. So what about the older orchards in existence? A few apple trees at the end of a garden will, in a good year, produce more apples than you can count. We have just had such a glut year. The country lanes have been full of fallen-down boxes outside neat cottage gates. The waterlogged sign on the heap of apples it once contained tells its own tale of plenty — 'apples for free: *please* take'. But in such a year of glut hardly anybody does. Our trees have produced mountains of apples and we have had a very hard struggle to keep up with them. We have produced tons of jelly and gallons of cider and wine. The jelly is now mostly sold and the cider and wine are maturing nicely. These are after all traditional products from the orchard. As are the sheep we fattened. They grazed on the windfalls and were fat by late September. We brought pailfuls of windfalls to the pigs and the chickens have scampered about — they like the apple seeds. There were times when the sheep were clearly overfaced with plenty. They started taking tiny bites from one apple before passing on to the next; the season slowed up though and they went back and cleared the hitherto neglected ones. Apple chutney, with added redcurrants left from jelly-making, was also produced in quantity. Next year there may well be a bad season and we will long for some of this year's crop. The few boxes of cookers that we have stored should last our own consumption for most of the winter. We did in fact try to sell some really beautiful cookers early in the season only to be told that there was no market at all. That is the whole story of country enterprise — if you cannot sell it as it is, convert it into something that does sell.

In Old Orchards a Fruit Picker is Often Safer than a Ladder

Pears are something that we would like to have more of. We have elderly trees that try their best but produce nothing of any real consequence. As we live in a fruit-producing district, we can buy pears very cheaply and turn them into chutney and wine. Although pears do make jam there never seems to be much demand for it. Perry used to be as widely made as cider in some districts and it is very light and delicate. Some orchards contain cherries and if you can get them before the birds, fresh cherries sell well almost every year. Cherry jam and chutneys are delicious: they sell well in specialist shops, but you must take the stones out. We turned pounds of beautiful dark red cherries into sweet chutney with peaches. We were thrilled to receive a letter of praise from a lady who lived hundreds of miles away who had bought a pot on holiday and taken it home. We were quite horrified, however, to learn that she had cracked a tooth on a stone. Although every effort had been made to remove them one had popped into her pot. This delightful person was not writing to complain or to claim her dentist's bills. She just thought that we might like to know for the next time. We have never felt quite committed about using cherries after that. Figs, apricots and other specialities can grow in some parts of Britain. All the different kinds of produce — jams, chutneys, wines and so on — can be used for these fruits although probably as they are something of a rarity growing in profusion in Britain, you would do as well to sell them locally, making sure that the public realises that they are locally grown and not imported.

THE VINEYARD

Less romantic than the orchard but equally desirable is a vineyard. In recent years vineyards have started sprouting up again in Britain. The Romans happily cultivated grapes in Britain not many years after Julius Caesar invaded us. Their growth prospered and became by tradition a part of the wealth of many monasteries. With Henry VIII's activities in that quarter, many vineyards fell into disrepair and viruses attacked the vines. In the nineteenth century it became popular among the landed gentry to grow grapes under glass. These were for family consumption and for impressing dinner guests. Great sums of money were spent on suitable glasshouses and gardeners' lives were dedicated to producing the finest and most succulent grapes. There were various necessities according to gardeners of the day. Whole bullocks were buried (dead ones, fortunately) under the vines to provide nourishment. If the carcass was not buried deeply enough, it often destroyed the vine. If it was planted deeply enough, it probably did no more good than a less horrifying application of bonemeal.

There is an imaginary line drawn from Pembroke to the Wash and if you live south of it, you can grow vines on south-facing slopes. If you live to the north of it, you require the additional shelter of a wall. In exposed areas the grapes will only ripen under glass. Grapes should be planted between October and March. The most successful transplants are usually one-year-old ones. The vines require staking and a top dressing of compost. The variety you choose should be governed first by the weather in your area and second by the type of grapes you wish to produce. On heavy soils you may well need to drain, using broken rubble or something similar. If you are fortunate enough to have an established vineyard in your area, you may be able to go on a tour of it. Here you can gather all sorts of valuable information. The varieties used, how they are trained, the work in progress on them and so on. Often vineyards sell young vines as part of their business; if the plants are growing well in your area, at least any questions about suitable hardiness are answered. Vineyards often use plastic netting as wind-breaks and for protection from frost. If you can keep an eye on a professional producer it makes your first few years easier.

Most grapes grown in the open end up as wine. You may wish to make the wine yourself or you may prefer to have it made for you. In our area there is one large producer who makes almost all the local wine. The grapes are harvested at the respective vineyards, transported, turned into wine and then returned to the vineyards where the wine is sold, directly and through retail outlets, as the produce of that vineyard. The problem with this kind of manufacture seems to be that as most of the grapes are of the same variety and the method of production is similar, the only possible major factor influencing the flavour is the soil itself. Although this certainly does produce variations it would be nice to have some other differences due to different manufacturers.

The Vineyard in November

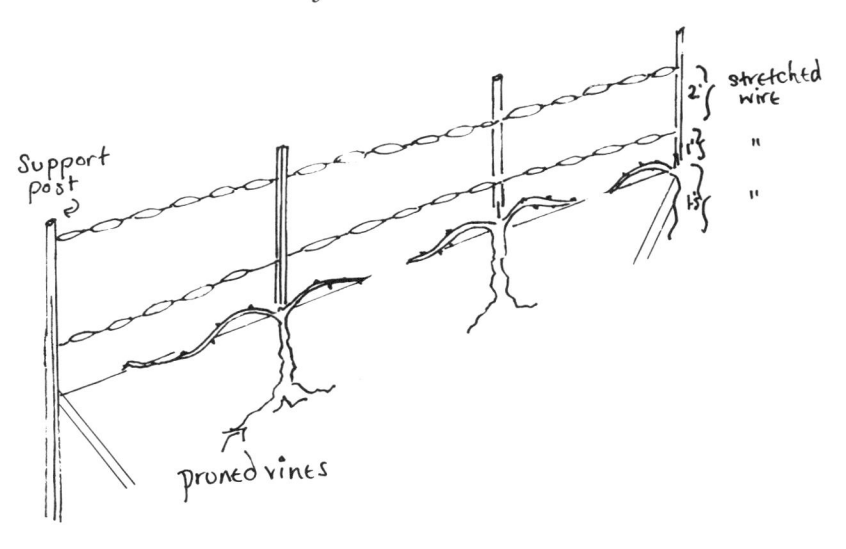

(diagram of pruned vines trained on stretched wire between support posts, with spacings labelled 2", 1½", 1½")

Grapes do still grow under glass today. We have a vine, some eighteen foot wide and very aged. We did not plant it ourselves and so cannot say with truth if it ever had a bullock planted to nourish it. However, it does do its own thing pretty well and with only a little care, produced well over a hundred pounds of grapes last Summer. To construct the size of greenhouse this vine needs today would be uneconomical. It certainly is delightful to be able to pick great bunches of delicious dessert grapes. We pickled some of them in vinegar with mustard and sold them as an accompaniment to Christmas ham. There is another slightly hidden crop from our grapevine. There are many more leaves produced than the vine needs. These make delicious dolmades, stuffed with rice, tomatoes, garlic and meat if you like. They also make a delicious addition to a salad or they can be cooked in a tomato-flavoured casserole with a large squeeze of lemon juice.

Woodlands

Going for walks in other people's woods is delightful — the trees are for climbing, admiring and possibly for carving your initials on. Going for walks in your own woods is rather different. It is more than likely that instead of admiring nature's generous hand, you will spend your time realising that you should not be walking at all. Rather you should be putting your wood in order. To be productive, and often simply to be penetrable, woodland needs maintaining. Left to its own devices, a wood quickly becomes tangled with fallen trees and rampant undergrowth and is a haven for foxes. If your aim is to encourage foxes then that is fine — if it is to grow trees then it is not.

In recent years many small parcels of woodland have fallen into a state of neglect. Woodland is often one of the first areas to feel a cutback in labour on large estates. Smaller landowners often tend to neglect woodland, possibly not appreciating that it is a potential income-producer. But if you are prepared to purchase a chainsaw and are able to wield it, remarkable feats can be performed in a short time. If you can enroll the help of family or friends, a veritable lumberjacking enterprise can be formed.

The first step towards taking control of existing woodland is to categorise it according to its function. There are four main types of woodland:

1. *Economic Woodland*. These are specific areas, planted, managed and farmed with the intention of producing quality timber.

2. *Amenity Woodland*. This includes single trees planted for their beauty, belts of woodland planted to conceal an unwanted view

such as farm buildings and clumps of woodland planted to enhance the landscape. The fact that these woodlands are required to be outwardly intact means that any felling must be staggered and replanting continuous.

3. *Shelter*. On some exposed properties belts of trees have been planted to provide shelter for land and/or buildings. Before any felling of trees takes place you must consider if this is the purpose for which they were planted. Trees take a long time to grow and shelter removed may well be regretted the instant the wind blows.

4. *Shooting Coverts*. These used to be planted simply to provide cover for game. Today this is quite uneconomic and new shooting coverts have to be planted with trees suitable to crop at some later stage. To fulfil the role of a covert, thought must be given not only to the size and shape of the wood but also to the layout (to provide rides and so on) and to ensure that the future work necessary in the wood will not interfere too much with the game. If you have to fulfil the dual role of woodsman and gamekeeper, you may find continual compromise a necessity. Different individuals performing the two roles will probably resort to the other alternative — argument.

There are three ways of planting:

1. *Coppice*. This is a short rotation system; poles grow from stools. Hazel coppice is the most widespread although today more use is made of chestnut coppice. Hazel is grown for hurdles and rods on a seven-year rotation. Chestnut, which is grown for fencing, is harvested on a fourteen-year cycle. If hop poles are the intended product, it may well take twenty years to grow them. The effect of coppice on the landscape is dynamic as in the harvesting year the wood is taken down to the stool. Very quickly masses of bluebells appear. However, within three or four years the area again resembles light forest.

2. *Coppice with Standards*. This is often produced when an owner has allowed his crop of coppice to grow on. Often this is because it is uneconomic to harvest it in his area. If this is the variety of woodland on your land, it is probably worth removing all but the

strongest shoot from each stool. This you can allow to grow on and cut later for fencing or turnery.

3. *High Forest*. This consists of trees grown to maturity with the aim of harvesting them when they are required. When they are required is generally when it suits the owner best from a tax point of view. Of course, when you are desperate you crop them at the earliest opportunity! This type of forest can either have been planted simultaneously with an aim of overall cropping or planted unevenly with an aim of staggered cropping. The latter method preserves the amenity value of the woodland.

If your aim is to take control of existing woodland then the best start is to categorise your wood according to its type and purpose. From there you can start to see an end-product.

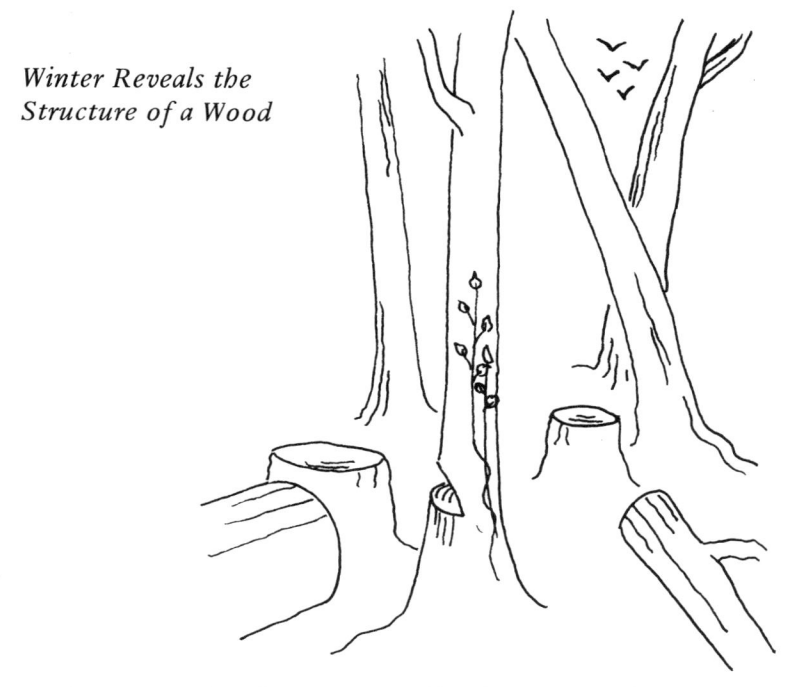

Winter Reveals the Structure of a Wood

If you are planning new woodland, you can choose the market you are aiming at. A specific variety of willow can be grown for cricket bats: these are most attractive trees for which you require a good soil with a high water content (not a marsh though). This is such a specialist area that you must establish if you have a market *before* you plant.

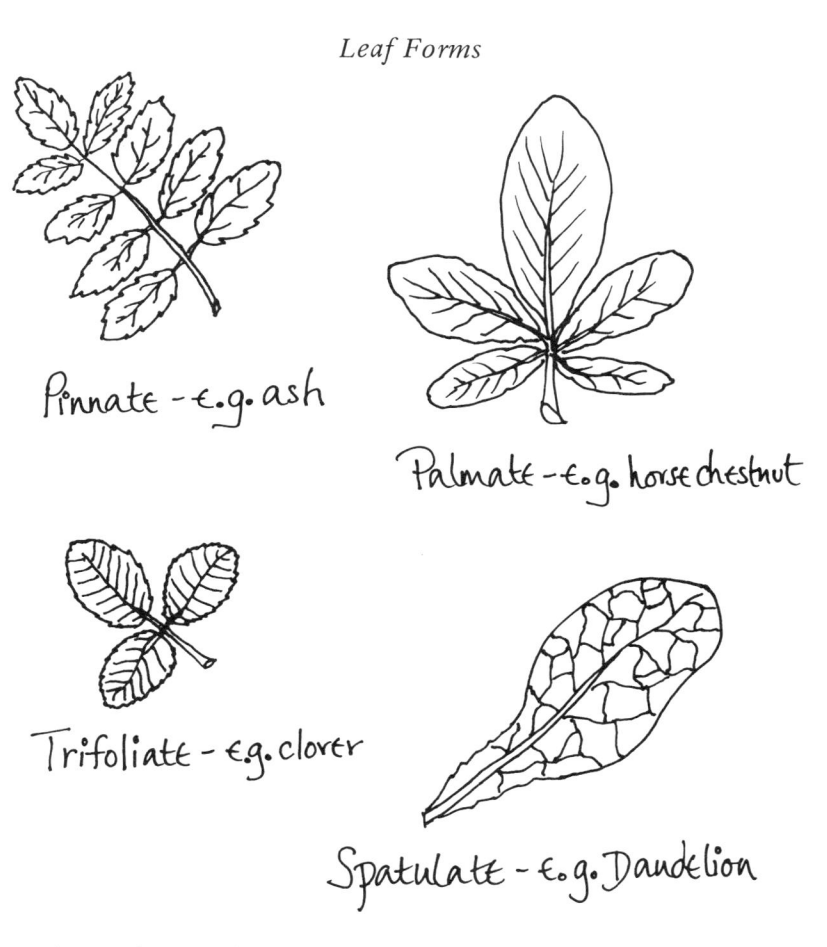

Leaf Forms

Pinnate – e.g. ash

Palmate – e.g. horse chestnut

Trifoliate – e.g. clover

Spatulate – e.g. Dandelion

It is worth considering growing 'instant trees' on a nursery scale. Developers and councils often have to purchase trees in an advanced stage of growth. Generally certain areas favour different varieties so some market research is needed. The trees have to be lifted very carefully and transport costs are high. However, well grown trees command a worthwhile return.

Christmas trees have an appeal all of their own. Everyone who plants them does so in a rosy glow of anticipation of a vast profit.

This is not the case for all who harvest them. To produce the ideal sought-after tree requires a lot of weeding or the branches do not spread out at the bottom. If you have to pay for this labour, the return on the trees is very small. Of course, a willing family can help a lot throughout the year. A good way to avoid the labour of harvesting the trees is to sell them on a 'pick your own' basis. This only works when you are reasonably near a centre of population: if you are it can be a great gimmick. It is very necessary to have adequate facilities for cars parking and turning, bearing in mind that most Christmases are wet. Purchasers who saw down their trees leave you with the work of removing the stump so it is well worth encouraging them to dig the whole thing up. As this is an occupation that removes father and children from the house for a considerable time during the Christmas rush, it is a good idea to slant your advertising towards the harrassed wife and mother. As people tend to be in a jolly mood at this time of year, it is worth having holly, mistletoe and perhaps also farm eggs available for sale. It seems that more and more people are reverting to a natural Christmas tree but bearing in mind the vast areas designated to their growth in remote areas, yours must be well shaped and reasonably priced to compete.

PLANTING NEW WOODLAND

Bearing in mind that faults in planting (poor transplants, cramped roots and so on) may take several years to show, planting is clearly a critical exercise. First, make a drawn plan of the area you intend to plant showing type, number and positioning of trees. From this plan, mark key points directly on the ground with pegs. It is essential that the transplants should be out of the ground for as short a time as possible and the roots must not be allowed to dry out in the meantime. The plants must be very well firmed in. The actual method of planting generally has to depend on the amount of labour available but it is well worth giving the small trees as good a start as possible. After all they may be going to grow on for a lot longer than you are. While the trees are very small they are at the mercy of sheep, deer, goats and other animals. A tasty mouthful for a goat is the total destruction of your effort. It is therefore well worth putting stockproof fencing around the wood. With the new woodland planted the aim is now to preserve and encourage it and a set routine is entered into.

1. *Weeding*. For the first few years it is necessary to weed the crop in the summer. Failure to do this means that many of the trees become stunted due to competition from brambles, weed seedlings and the like. The weeding must not be performed too enthusiastically as the plants suffer from sunscorch if they are totally denuded of cover. This is where it becomes more difficult if you use chemical weeders as they tend to leave the ground absolutely clean.

2. *Beating Up*. This rather hearty expression merely means replacing any plants that have withered and died. The gaps have to be filled with strong-growing plants or else their neighbours grow above them and the newcomers are stunted.

3. *Cleaning*. This takes place after the canopy has closed. This is the time to remove any tree weeds — ones you did not plant. Also remove any overenthusiastic ones that you did — you are aiming for even growth.

4. *Brashing*. This is lopping off spreading side branches that do not allow you to walk through the wood. It only has to be done to just above head height and you may only wish to clear paths, not the whole wood.

5. *Pruning*. To obtain fine, clean timber, prune before the butt is more than four feet in diameter. This is not always done today as it is a very labour-intensive procedure. For special trees such as the cricket bat willow it is essential.

6. *Thinning*. As the forest grows it needs thinning. Fast maturing varieties may require thinning every three years, others every five. Thinning does not start until about the twelfth year of growth. There are tables to check by height, age and diameter how many trees need to be removed.

ESTABLISHED WOODLAND

When woodland is established, the aim is to manage it to produce saleable timber while preserving any other roles the area has to perform. There are many sources of advice available to this end. Government officials and private companies specialise in forestry and timber. The Timber Growers Association will give information on reliable contractors and markets in your area. The Forestry Commission will advise you on extradition licences and necessary permissions to obtain before you fell. It is certainly worth taking all the advice you can obtain on reliable purchasers in your area. Timber seems to be an area where there are a great many small 'cowboys' working. We have had some astonishingly different offers for standing timber and most people who sell timber have had similar experiences. Timber is sold either standing or felled. When buying standing timber, the merchant will clearly leave himself a margin for possible unsound butts. If you have felled the timber, this will generally increase the price. Privately grown timber is generally sold by private treaty; usually only very large organisations can succeed in successfully auctioning timber. If you obtain several offers for your timber, you can take the most competitive offer. This is not always the one that offers you the most money. Wood is unbelievably heavy. If moved without due care and attention, it can cause a great deal of damage to land, other trees and so on. This, of course, costs you money to repair. Extra heavy vehicles on farm roads can cause subsidence, another costly repair job. All these details have to be worked out before the deal is completed. It is then essential to draw up a contract specifying extraction routes, clearing dates, how and when you will be paid and what compensation is payable in the event of damage. This should be signed by both sides. It should also contain a clause specifying that the timber is yours until paid for. This saves you unending hassle should the firm go bankrupt.

Dedicated Woodland

This is often advertised for sale. It is exactly what it says: dedicated. Basically, the land is under covenant to be kept as woodland for ever. This means that felling can only be practised when replanting is also practised. This procedure was started in 1947 with the aim of increasing and maintaining the growth and production of timber in Britain.

The Approved Woodland Scheme

In 1952 this scheme was added to the procedure for dedicated woodland. If an owner did not wish to dedicate his woodland in perpetuity, he could agree to manage it with a plan of operations approved by the Forestry Commission.

Small Woods Scheme

The aim of this scheme is to further encourage planting and timber management. It applies to small areas of woodland that are not suitable for the first two schemes, for example individual blocks of woodland of less than five acres.

All the above schemes entitle the owner of the woodland to Planting and Management grants. Further information is available from your local Forestry Commission District Officer. Of course, the aim of all the schemes is to encourage the managed growth of one of our national assets: good timber.

BY-PRODUCTS

Having a wood in a timber-producing situation also provides other crops. The most obvious of these is firewood.

Firewood

In almost every system of forestry firewood is produced. Casualty trees, early thinnings and thick prunings all produce it. If you are near a centre of population, advertising a delivery service of seasoned, cut logs can produce a good trade. In some areas, it is possible to encourage car-boot sales. Your customers can fill their boot for a few pounds and you save on the delivery costs and effort. Dry access is essential. As in all dealings with the public a little thought goes a long way. Friends of ours ordered a ton of logs from a pleasant couple of youngsters who canvassed their business. The stipulation was that the logs were to be unloaded at the rear of the garage in the dry. Our likely lads came to deliver when no-one was at home. They deposited the load as close to the planned delivery point as they could get it, right up against the closed garage door. The whole family spent a furious Saturday morning removing the logs so that they could get the car out of the garage and then loading the logs into the rear. No repeat orders there! Wood-burning stove customers are certainly worth wooing as they consume great quantities of wood every year. Of course, if you are not near anyone who wants your logs, you will have to become your own best customer. How about heating acres of glasshouses with a wood-fired boiler?

Leafmould

This is another crop from woodland. Well decayed leafmould packed into heavy-duty polythene bags can sell Farm Gate. If it is attractively packed, you can try local garden centres and so on.

Greenery

Attractive and seasonal greenery such as holly and ivy can sell Farm Gate or to vegetable retailers at Christmas. It is also possible to sell laurel and pine trimmings to florists.

Fencing

With some simple equipment such as a chainsaw and machete, rustic fencing can be produced. As most fencing is sold for an aesthetic purpose, it must have a regular appearance. Practise on your own fencing first!

Rustic Furniture

This is most popular in rural areas. Its use in towns seems to depend upon current trends. All kinds of objects can be made: tables, chairs, benches, even bridges. Being able to display your goods to the public is very useful; quite often nurseries and garden centres will display goods on a commission basis which is very helpful if your own property is unsuitable for this.

Sheep

Keeping sheep is very rewarding. They are gentle creatures, providing us with playful lambs to watch in the spring, that finest of fibres, wool, and finally with delicious lamb and mutton. They also eat grass like lawn-mowers and kindly scatter their droppings finely all over the field — they are natural muck-spreaders. Depending on breed, sheep will thrive on thick luscious grassland, slowly nibbling away their days while remaining happily within their boundaries, or they will survive on rough moorland with the wind whistling around their thick fleeces, acknowledging no man-made boundaries. At least they are quite territorially minded on the moors and establish their own range.

The first stage in sheep-keeping is to match your available grazing with a suitable breed. Having chosen a breed, you can go to a market and bid for some or find a farmer who breeds to sell. The latter course is definitely preferable. For a start, you can get a lot of good advice about sheep by listening to practising farmers. You can also take a good look at your prospective sheep while they are carrying out their natural occupation — eating grass. The sheep you buy will not have suffered the stresses of having gone to market, been unloaded, penned and reloaded. Also, and this is very important, they will not have come into contact with a lot of other sheep (potential bug-carriers). *Farmers Weekly* carries advertisements of sheep for sale as do some local papers. Breed societies can put you in touch with potential suppliers as well. If you choose a breed that is not specific to your area, you may have to travel a fair distance to get your sheep. It is worth remembering that unless you are providing your own transport, the cost of transporting the sheep will probably be higher than your own.

Sheep are referred to in terms of age and sex. Farmers are always willing to translate but here are a few of the more usual terms:

Females

Birth to weaning	*Ewe lamb*
Weaning to first shear	*Ewe teg*
First shear to second shear	*Gimmer*
Has lambed at least once	*Ewe*

Males — entire

Birth to first shearing	*ram lamb*
First shear and on	*Shearing tup*
Then numbered by shearing, i.e.	2 shear tup

Males — castrated

Weaning to first shear	*Wether*
After first shear	*Shearing wether*

Very few castrated males are kept after their first shear as they have no use other than grass mowing or being kept as pets.

For a first exercise in sheep-keeping, it is probably worth buying ewes that have already lambed at least once. This way at least one of you has had some experience! The very first sheep we bought many years ago had just lambed. We therefore had an easy introduction, it was a mild Spring and the dear little lambs obligingly gambolled about as their dams contentedly grazed. It was almost enough to contradict the opinion of many sheep-owners — that sheep are just wandering about waiting for an excuse to die. This sounds a bit odd but in fact sheep do seem to have less will to live than most other animals. Anyway, our lambs grew well and the ewes ate their way towards Autumn. We brought in rams and the cycle started again. We kept on the ewe lambs for breeding and sold the castrated ram lambs to friends with freezers.

Lamb is the simplest meat to sell. It is a small carcass compared to pork or beef and is easily jointed and transported. When the sheep are big enough you take them to a slaughter-house to be killed. You then collect them. Some slaughter-houses will joint and pack for you; they charge for it, of course — some a lot more than others. If you feel too much of your profit is going in their charges, it is not difficult to joint and pack yourself. There are full instructions on pages 146-7. If you let the weight of the meat 'help' you, there is very little 'strong-arm technique' required. When you produce a lot of lamb the extra profit is considerable. When the lamb is slaughtered the skin is usually taken as part of the fee. This is all very well unless you want to cure the skin. Some slaughter-houses will not let you have your skins back: it is too difficult for them to differentiate with the numbers they handle. We keep quite a lot of Jacob sheep and like to have all our skins so we have to travel a fair distance to a suitable slaughter-house. In fact, some slaughter-houses will not accept Jacobs at all so you must check first if you have some ready. Warning! When you get the skin back you will also get the head. *Never* feed this to a dog: there is a worm that forms a cyst in sheep's heads that if passed on to dogs is very unpleasant indeed.

JACOBS

These are such a popular breed for keeping on a small scale that they deserve a special mention. They are often advertised for sale in local papers and Jacob rams are often available for loan during the breeding season. Some years ago they were in danger of extinction but now, due mainly to the efforts of the Jacob Sheep Society, they are our most widely available 'exotic' sheep. We have kept Jacobs for ten years and ours have descended down to great, great . . . granddaughters. We have greatly enjoyed watching the inherited characteristics pass on. Our first lead sheep was an aged ewe called Frosty. Her fleece was a most beautiful mixture of soft greys and browns. Her legs were immaculately striped like football socks and she held her aristocratic head obstinately high. She was an expert at removing herself and her flock from wherever you had put them. She treated electric fencing with utter disdain and she and her followers cavorted high in the air over it. We never did the trick of holding her sensitive mouth around the wire so that she would get a strong shock. Our feelings were governed by a mixture of sympathy with her and conviction that as she jumped it clear every time it would make no difference anyway. No doubt there are many who remember the hills and valleys of Kent echoing to plaintive cries of 'No, Frosty, no'. Those days are now gone and Frosty remains only in our memory. It is quite an anticlimax when our present flock trots off happily where we send them; there are, however, still a sprinkling of football socks among the youngsters.

A Fine Jacob Ram Will Guard his Flock — and Eat your Apples if Allowed to!

Jacobs are very attractive, give excellent coloured wool, usually drop twins and provide superb lamb and mutton. As with most unusual things, a lot was said against Jacob meat in the early days. The main complaint concerned the smallness of the joints but it has to be said that as the bones are particularly light, they carry a higher proportion of meat than most other breeds and that is after all what we eat. The meat is absolutely lean and quite delicious; even Jacob mutton has a fine texture. We have sold the meat widely and customers always come back for more. Last year we ran a Dorset Horn ram with some of our ewes. This has fattened our lambs and made the joints larger; this increases our profit but in fact we still prefer the Jacob meat ourselves. The ewe lambs from this cross were most attractive — mainly chocolate brown with a white tail and white face markings. The ram lambs were somewhat mottled and their curly Dorset horns look quite odd on the speckled coat. We have run our Jacob rams with white sheep — mainly Kents. The resulting lambs are black and heavier than the Jacobs; they seem to inherit the forwardness of the Jacobs and are more inquisitive than their mothers. Jacob rams tend to be very enthusiastic and as they possess considerable jumping powers they can be a problem. We had a neighbour whose Jacob ram leapt a vast fence to join some glamorous white ewes one Autumn. The ram was there all night before he was discovered. We all waited with baited breath for the following Spring — the neighbour in fear of a massive paternity suit, the farmer imagining a holiday in the Bahamas on the proceeds. We built even higher fences around our rams. Spring came and there was not a single black lamb. Presumably the Jacob ram had been too exhausted by his leap to accomplish anything more.

WOOL

Almost every sheep is clipped by electric shears. If you intend to do this yourself, if is definitely worth being shown the technique by an expert. It is very easy to cut the sheep's skin. Agricultural Colleges often hold day-courses in sheep-shearing and lambing. You can also clip using sheep shears; these require strong wrists and care in use. Skilled users can clip astonishingly quickly with them. You can also clip with large sharp scissors: this, although unorthodox, is extremely effective.

Sheep are shorn in the early summer when the wool starts to lift. When you push some of the fleece away so that you reveal the skin, you can see a thinner band in the wool just above the skin. This is where you cut. The fleece should come off in one great piece to be rolled and tied. If you put the sheep on to clean concrete for shearing or failing that on to a clean sheet or something similar, you will keep the fleeces clean. This is especially important if you are intending to hand-spin the fleece or to sell it to someone who is. It is always amusing to see the goat-like creature that emerges from the sheep's fleece. Within a few days they look fairly normal again, but initially even the sheep move around somewhat furtively in their new freedom.

The wool is a valuable product. If you have more than four sheep and intend to sell the wool, you can legally only sell it to the Wool Marketing Board. Unlike everything else, the price you will obtain has not altered dramatically in recent times and your wool will certainly seem undervalued. You can, of course, split the ownership of the sheep around the family: four for Mother, four for Father, four for each of the children. Craft shops often buy good fleeces as, of course, hand-spinners will. There are a few suggestions for further uses of wool in Chapter 19. It is worth repeating: wool is valuable. After all, one fleece could produce a jumper, hat and gloves for each member of a family of four; unfortunately, when a monetary value is put on the fleece, this never seems to be reflected.

RAM MANAGEMENT

If you intend to buy or hire a ram, look carefully at his records. If he is unproven (in his first working year), look at his parents' records. Make sure he is healthy, of a good build and, if possible, see that he knows what the job is about. Putting a ram in with your flock in November will give you lambs in April. When you want your lambs depends on two factors: the first concerns whether you are lambing indoors or out and the second concerns the usual weather conditions in your area. If you live on top of a mountain and are not prepared to feed mother and lambs until Spring really comes it is better to lamb late. If you live in a delightfully sheltered spot with early Springs, you can lamb very early and catch the premium lamb market. Ewes come into season in the autumn and if not successfully mated, they return every 16-18 days. The ram should run with them for at least six weeks to cover two seasons. It makes life a lot easier if the ram wears a raddle. This is basically a coloured marker tied to his chest that rubs off on to the ewe when she is served. Changing the colour after a couple of weeks means that you can follow the progress. When a ewe is coloured twice it means that she has not held to the first service. With a few sheep you can work out pretty closely when the lambs should arrive. With more, the lambing is spread over a longer period.

WINTER

When the grazing falls off, you must supplement the sheep's roughage with hay. It is worth feeding the ewes well for this affects the lambs' growth and birth numbers. Not too well though; fat animals of any species find giving birth more difficult. A mineral block should be in the field at all times and some concentrate is needed. How much depends on the sort of supplement you choose and the quality of the hay. Sheep tend to eat up fairly quickly so if you find any food left over in the trough then you are feeding too much.

  We leave our rams running with the flock for most of the winter. We work on the theory that the rams see dogs and foxes off. The most docile family dog can turn killer. Dogs in groups seem to revert to their wolf-like ancestors. Hopefully you will never come across a sheep that has been mauled by a dog. If you do you will understand why many farmers shoot dogs on sight that are roaming in their fields. Dogs do not even have to catch the sheep to harm them. Sheep are timid and if chased, even if the dog is only intending to play, they are convinced of an imminent end. The ewes lose lambs that they are carrying and hurl themselves into danger. We live near the River Medway and every year a few sheep meet a watery end trying to escape from dogs.

If you have a suitable building (an airy pole barn is ideal), it is worth considering inwintering the sheep. Many more farmers are practising this today, both for the higher lambing percentages and for the comfort of the shepherd. Your enemy with sheep in confinement is condensation: sheep like fresh air, not damp air. There have been noticeable rises in birth weights when the ewes have been sheared on coming in. There is the added benefit that your land gets a total rest through the winter and Spring growth will therefore be more lush. Apart from feeding hay and concentrates, it may be worth considering feeding silage or hydroponically grown grass. Sheep can thrive on silage but should be introduced to it gradually, preferably while they are still grazing the fields. Hydroponic grass is fantastically popular with housed sheep. The only problem is not to overfeed them with it or they may scour.

SPRING

The main aim through the preceding months has been to bring the ewe to lambing in a fit — not fat — condition, with her lambs healthy and well grown. If your ewes have not been inwintered, they should come in now. It is certainly worth spending time and effort to provide yourself with a building to lamb in. Even a temporary shelter of straw bales close to the house makes a great difference. If you ever have to attend to a ewe which is lambing in an exposed field in the early hours of the morning, with the wind howling and the hurricane lamp flickering, you will recognise the appeal of lambing indoors. If your vet has to accompany you on your cold mission, he will certainly add weight to the cause.

To get the most live lambs — and that is what it is all about — you want to be in pretty constant attendance. If the ewe drops her lambs cleanly and enthusiastically licks them dry, all you have to do is watch to see that the lambs suckle. If the ewe struggles for a while and is in obvious discomfort then call the vet, unless you have had a lot of experience in lambing yourself. Twin lambs can get tangled up inside the ewe, a lamb's head can get jammed backwards — all kinds of difficulties can prevent the ewe from an unaided delivery. Putting a hand into the ewe to help is only successful if you can identify what you have hold of and this is astonishingly difficult. When the vet helps he generally gives the ewe an antibiotic in case an infection sets in. Sometimes the lambs that arrive are very dopey and if the mother does not lick them hard enough you must take all the mucus from around the lamb's nose and face. A good rub with a rough towel is often enough to get the little one going. When a lamb is really cold and not reacting, the most effective life-saving operation is to warm it up. For years the traditional way to do this has been to pop it in front of the fire or in the cool oven of the Aga — with the door open! We have revived all sorts of apparently hopeless creatures this way. There are now quite a few gadgets available without resorting to the kitchen: most work on a kind of boxed-in hairdrier theory.

It is worth checking before lambing that the lambs will have good access to the milk. Long straggly wool near the udder should be clipped away or lambs may suck on this instead of continuing to look for the real thing. A lamb that is slow in going for milk will receive encouraging butts in its bottom from an experienced ewe; if your ewe is not bothering, pat the lamb's rear yourself. Once a lamb is going well on the teat that should be the end of problems. A lamb that for some reason is removed totally from its mother must still have colostrum (the first milk). It is perfectly satisfactory to give it some from another newly lambed ewe. In fact, it freezes quite well so you can have a stock on hand. You can tell colostrum by its appearance: it is thick and yellow. Normal sheep's milk looks pretty much like cow's milk. The colostrum contains essential antibodies for the lamb's protection and lambs that do not receive it are much more liable to infection. Once a lamb has been totally removed from its mother you either have to persuade another ewe to be Mum or do it yourself. The main cause of rejection from a new ewe will be smell. Sometimes you can confuse the ewe by spraying perfume over her face and then over the lamb. We have a friend who practises this method using overwhelming wafts of Chanel No. 5. What ever the vet thinks when he visits he does not say. Neither does he say if his wife believes why he smells so exotic!

When you have tried all the tricks and are still faced with a hungry lamb, you must resort to the bottle. Feeding lambs is a delightful pastime unless you have other things that must be done. Every year we have to fight our daughter who would happily feed dozens of them. To start with, a baby's bottle is big enough — just do not give it back to the baby! Soon you will need something bigger. Teats and substitute milk are available from some agricultural merchants and Boots' Farm Sales. Lambs will thrive on goat's milk but it is not advisable to let them suckle directly as their natural butting at the udder can damage the goat's large milk vessel. Many bottle-fed lambs go on to become family pets. They will follow you around even when they are fully grown. This is quite satisfactory with ewes; it is not so acceptable with rams. Bottle-fed ram lambs should be destined for the freezer. They are too casual with you and can be dangerous when fully grown. Even those breeds without horns can deliver a hefty blow and with horns, the possibilities are endless.

To castrate ram lambs and to dock the tails of lowland lambs, the most usual method is to use very tight heavyweight elastic bands. These bands and the applicator come from agricultural suppliers. It is advisable to dock the tails of sheep that will feed on good pasture as it prevents the area around the tail from becoming clogged with droppings that are soft from the rich grazing. If this area is dirty, it attracts flies to lay their eggs. These hatch into maggots which start eating the sheep. This revolting occurrence is referred to as an attack of strike. If you ever see it you will spend a lot of your sheep-keeping life trying to avoid it. It is very unpleasant indeed.

SUMMER

Now the lambs are growing at an astonishing rate. The ewes are grazing their way on to another year of production. Wool is shorn and sold. The continuous movement of sheep around the holding is practised as in the 'sheep health' section to prevent a build-up of parasites.

Stocking rates

3 ewes with two lambs each: best seeds pasture — 1 acre.
2 ewes with three lambs between them: normal pasture — 1 acre.
1 ewe with one lamb: good hill grass — 1 acre.
1 ewe with one lamb: poor mountain — 5 to 10 acres.

All the above stocking rates assume reasonable weather. In a very dry year the sheep may need more grass. There should always be a mineral lick available.

LATE SUMMER/AUTUMN

Fat lambs should be sold as soon as they are ready. Cull ewes (unproductive, barren ones) should be sold as mutton while they are still fat from the summer grass. Dipping should be carried out.

Now the whole year's cycle starts again.

SHEEP'S MILK

There is information about milking sheep and how to use the milk on pages 129, 133 and 167-71. Sheep's milk is regaining the popularity it once had: many of the cheeses we eat today made from cow's milk were originally produced from the milk of sheep. This is often referred to as the third profit from sheep-keeping.

SHEEP HEALTH

An all-important aspect of sheep management is to know your animals and to be able to recognise when problems occur. Normally a sheep will breathe at the rate of 15-20 respirations per minute. Lambs will breathe more rapidly as will ruminating animals. However, any marked increase in the rate or ragged breathing is usually an indication of trouble. The normal pulse rate is four times the respiratory rate. The easiest place to find a pulse on a sheep is half way down the inside of a rear leg. The normal temperature for a sheep is 103-105°F. Young animals have slightly higher temperatures as do animals which have been exercising. A raised temperature is often accompanied by a fever. A low temperature can occur when an animal is haemorrhaging.

Faeces and urine are good indicators of a sheep's state of health. Any change of colour or smell that is not caused by a change in feeding should be suspected as the sign of a problem. Young grass often causes sheep to scour, usually this can be cured by feeding hay.

The Ultimate — a Flock of Alert, Healthy Sheep

The initial requirement of a lamb is colostrum, this gives the lamb natural immunity to many diseases. If a ewe is vaccinated against dysentry she will pass immunity to the lamb via her milk for several weeks. From this early age the lamb is subject to attack from worms it eats from the grass. Worm eggs will last for a long time on grazed fields, to be quite safe fields should be rested for six-month periods, this of course is not always possible but at least some rotation should be practised to break the pattern of sheep eating worm eggs, worms forming inside the sheep or more eggs passing out in droppings. Sheep should be wormed regularly, how often depends on the system you choose. The simplest is to add granules of wormer to a feed of grain, the problem here is that the weaker sheep eat less of the grain and may not receive the necessary dose. An injector gun is very effective. A pouch filled with liquid wormer is attached to the shepherd and holding the gun, western style, you can effectively dose a lot of sheep in a short time. It has been known for the shepherd to worm himself in this operation — the needle is unpleasantly large but there do not seem to be any after effects! There are some diseases that occur regularly in specific areas, so it is worth asking your vet if there are any specific precautions you should take in your area.

Dipping is generally compulsory now. The choices at dipping

start with whether you intend to do it yourself or have it done for you. There are contractors who will arrive at your flock and do the whole thing for you. In our area you have to have at least 60 sheep to make this an economic operation; of course you can always gather a few owners together if you cannot make up that number yourself. Sometimes local farmers will let you take your sheep to be dipped along with theirs in a fixed dipping setup. Otherwise you must look to your own resources. A fibreglass dip tank with an organised run makes the whole affair move with clockwork precision. Putting the sheep one after another by hand into a tank is heavy work. From experience we would point out that getting the wet sheep out of the tank requires superhuman effort. The sheep must be totally immersed but they must not be overstressed. Quite often it is a useful thing to have at least one more pair of hands than you expect to need at a time like this.

Sheep also require maintenance of their feet and tail areas. The feet must be carefully trimmed and kept in good condition to avoid footrot. The area around the tail should be kept trimmed and clean from wet droppings or you may find yourself with an attack of strike. Flies lay eggs in the matted wool, these hatch and the maggots start to eat the sheep. It sounds revolting and is. Prevention is far better than cure.

Beef

Beef produced slowly, maturing, not being forced: this is what produces the beautiful marbled meat which is glowingly described in gastronomic textbooks. Most of the beef we eat today has been encouraged to grow at speed. A lot of it was encouraged to grow by being injected with steroids. The moment the carcass is big enough to market it is off. Very often the traditional 'finishing' stage — the stage which produces the rounded carcass, the marbled meat — is missed out or skimped on. In the 1960s there was a great fashion for producing and eating baby beef. These small joints came from animals totally intensively fattened and killed at under a year. Although the rising price of cereal makes it unlikely for this to happen again there is clearly a great attraction in moving the animals as quickly as possible.

In any enterprise where you consider rearing and producing beef, the first fact to consider is that it is the slowest livestock enterprise to produce your profit. There are, of course, stages at which you can get in and out of the market but generally the major profit goes to the person with the animal at the end of the process. Using a semi-intensive system, this means at the end of an eighteen-month period. Or it could mean a two-year animal. Very rarely does anyone go on for any longer than that.

How you start depends on whether you have bred the calf yourself or whether you are buying in. With a dairy cow operation there are surplus calves to put into beef production. You could run some cows simply for their calves; these run with their dams and require the least effort of all calves. It is more likely that the enterprise starts with buying in calves. Calves are beautiful little creatures but the important thing to bear in mind is that one day they will be enormous, not so friendly and require space and a great deal of food. It is essential that a calf receives colostrum. If you buy direct from the producer, you can ask for a guarantee that it has. If you buy from the market, you have no such certainty. To produce beef easily you require a beef breed. Every bovine animal will produce some beef when killed; the beef breeds produce the right amount in the right places. Hereford crosses are traditionally excellent; also good are Friesian bull calves, and Aberdeen Angus which thrive on low-grade pasture. The safest way to get the best animal for your area is to have a look and see what everyone else is doing. If the fields around you are stocked with Herefords, have a go with them. There is no point in putting a Charolais that requires good grazing to fatten on land that would better accommodate the less fussy Aberdeen Angus.

Bucket Feeding for Calves — the Easy Way

rubber teat

When the calf first arrives you have to teach it to drink from the bucket. This can be very difficult with awkward calves who dislike the possibility of being drowned in the bucket. You can make it very easy by adapting your bucket to take the teat feeders available at agricultural suppliers. We turned to these in desperation one cold winter when we had a batch of Charolais crosses.

For some reason they were the most awkward feeders. The usual thing is to gently lead the calf's muzzle down into the milk with your fingers. The calf will happily suck your fingers: after all they are very like Mother's milk dispensers. These calves all grabbed on to your fingers, bit the backs of them with their sharp-edged teeth, then butted in furiously to give the signal for the milk to start flowing. All that did to chapped fingers was to start the blood flowing! The monsters were madly enthusiastic about the teat system. The problem was to fasten the buckets so that their butting did not send the milk up into the air. Anyway our hands recovered and now we feed all the calves this way. The calves are fed on reconstituted dried milk. This is cheaper than whole milk even if you produce the milk. You can sell the milk you produce for more. If you have Channel Island cows and for some reason have to feed their milk to calves, you must dilute it with water. About a third as much water as milk is generally sufficient. If you do not, the calves will scour as the milk is so rich. This is even the case if you feed Channel Island milk to Channel Island calves.

Naturally Polled Charolais — this could be the shape of champion beef bulls of the future

The calves are weaned on to a cereal mix. The simplest way to buy this is pre-mixed from an agricultural merchant. In the spring if you bought an Autumn calf, or late Summer if you bought a Spring one, you can turn the young stock out. The grass they go on to should not have been grazed by other livestock for a long time. If the last livestock was cattle, there should ideally have been a twelve-month gap. If it was sheep, a few months is sufficient. These animals are extremely susceptible to infection at this stage and every effort should be made to minimise worm loads on fields and flies in the area. If the weather is unkind, they may well require gradual hardening off, like plants. In any case, they will still need some concentrate until they get used to their new diet. If they were put out in the spring, they can stay out well into September. If you put them out in August, you only have a month or so before they come back in. Inside, they are fed on silage or hay and barley to keep them in a growing condition. Depending on breed, the animals can finish indoors on this ration or go out on to the spring grass and then finish at the end of the summer. They are happiest in batches of about ten when they are indoors and you must always be careful that none of them gets left behind in growth. If they do, it is best to separate the slow ones off. The animals that finish on grass always seem to have a better flavour. However, animals out in fields are exposed to poisoning and other hazards so they are usually sent off as soon as they reach the required weight. This is around 500 kg depending on breed. That just goes to show how much calves grow. A batch of ten tiny calves grows to a joint weight of around 5,000 kg. That is a lot of beef.

Pigs

Pigs are intelligent, likeable characters. They are individuals by nature and unlike their reputations will be extremely clean if they are allowed to be. Given enough space they will conveniently deposit their dung in one prescribed area, leaving their bedding clean. When they are crammed together and are unable to do this they start to look like the fabled 'dirty' pig.

There are two basic methods of pig production: intensive and extensive. Taken to extremes, intensive can mean production on a battery scale. Litters of piglets can be removed from the sow very shortly after birth to be reared in 'flat decks' on sow milk substitute and then weaned at a very early age. The sow is put back in pig as quickly as possible. The aim is to achieve as close to three litters a year as is possible. This kind of production is extremely capital-intensive and also the subject of much concern as to the welfare of the animals. The main motivation for this kind of development has been the low profit per head of bacon or pork pigs.

For a small producer the answer has to be to produce absolutely top-grade pigs and also to catch a premium market. Our pork pigs have always been extremely lean and we have sold mainly to the home-freezer market. When we have produced pigs surplus to our orders, the slaughter-house has happily bought them because of our good gradings. Our production is not on a battery scale. Our dry sows live together in threes in kennel-type buildings made of concrete blocks; these have outside areas where they dung and inside the kennels are liberally bedded with straw. When it is fairly dry the sows eat outside, when it is wet they eat inside. They are given plenty of trough room. Pigs do like to eat and will fight viciously if they feel deprived. We clean the outside dunging areas morning and evening. That way there is little dung to remove and the work is speedy. Also it keeps the pigs clean and contented. They have constant clean water available. Weaners thrive on a similar regime. (Weaners are pigs that have left their dams and are in the process of growing on either as more breeding stock or as potential pork pigs.) We keep weaners in batches of eight to ten. We have tried using a covered building to avoid wet feeding in the rain but we soon found that the pigs were much more susceptible to infection and we also disliked the unbelievable shrieking they all set up at feed-time.

Sow in Farrowing Crate With Twelve Piglets

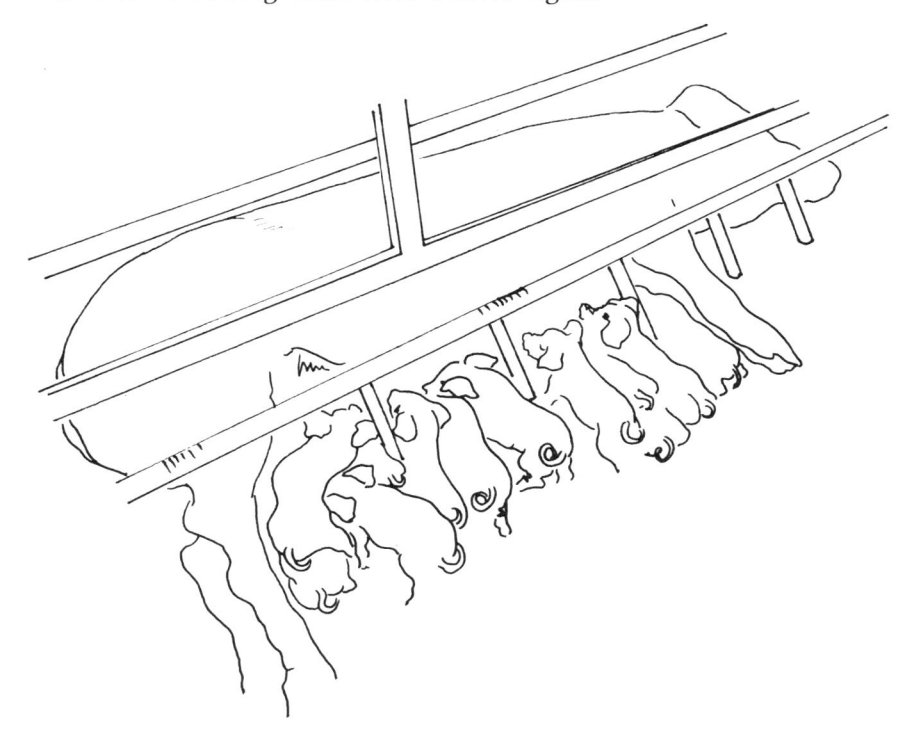

We have very few calls from the vet and these are almost entirely limited to when a sow or gilt is farrowing (giving birth). A farrowing house is essential if you have more than a very few sows. With one or two you could use a stable or similar building. The main aim is to have the area as germ-free as possible and to provide adequate protection for the piglets. The protection is mainly from their mother. A large sow is an unwieldy creature and as she is producing up to eleven tiny piglets the odds of her squashing one or two are quite high. To prevent this, many births take place in a farrowing crate. These are metal crates that restrain the pig from turning round and keep her confined during the birth. We use them as there does not really seem to be any other satisfactory way. They are also extremely useful if the vet has to render assistance. A boar pen is the last necessary building. A boar should be housed on its own but fairly close to the females you want him to serve. This encourages the females to come on heat.

We only run a few pigs extensively as our land is heavy clay and therefore cold and wet. Pigs thrive best on exactly the opposite soil, one that is well drained and warm. Pigs kept in fields in arcs — those tin-covered huts, rather like miniature Nissen huts — require plenty of warm straw for bedding and supplementary food. They will take some food from the grass but this is not sufficient. Some pigs breed out in their huts, the major drawback here being that if there are difficulties it is extremely hard to deal with an unrestrained pig and, of course, since many births occur at night, you have the dark as well as the wind and rain with which to contend. Having said all that, it is a fact that piglets who live out with their mothers tend to thrive. Because they have free access to the ground and its inherent minerals, they do not need the injections of iron that indoor-reared piglets must have. Probably the best compromise if your land is suitable for running pigs is to breed them in confinement and gradually introduce them to the open air.

The facility that pigs have of rooting into the ground can be a menace or a blessing. It is a menace if you are intending to run them on grass fields: you then have to put rings through their noses or they will effectively plough up your grassland for you. Of course, if you have some scrubland that you want cleared, their labour is a great help: in go roots, leaves, fallen apples and so on and out comes an excellent manure. You could even plant a tasty root crop for the pigs to dig for and in their search they will effectively rotivate and fertilise; however, they will still need some supplementary food. Pig food comes in one of two forms: one is a mixture of grain, added-protein fishmeal or something similar, and necessary vitamins and minerals; the other is swill. Swill used to be the great money-maker in the pig business. In some areas it may well still be. However, it is, of course, waste food and is a potential spreader of disease to pigs. It is thought that several of the particularly virulent pig diseases are spread this way. There is a legal requirement that all swill is boiled for at least one hour. The immense boilers necessary on large farms are often horrifying in appearance. Total effectiveness is necessary and this includes a routine that prevents the contamination of boiled swill by proximity to newly arrived swill. If you are only processing your own household swill the problems are not so enormous; even so, when you realise that if you eat bought bacon and leave a rind it is a potential source of infection to your own pigs, it is clear that even this must be well boiled.

BREEDS OF PIGS

Many years ago pigs were selected and bred for their beauty. There are some staggeringly fat pigs in nineteenth-century paintings; with the quantity of fat on those creatures you can certainly see why Jack Sprat's wife was the fat one. Today pigs have been bred to be leaner — almost everyone prefers lean pork; in fact, the ideal pig would have an extremely long back and four rear legs. When you sell meat the reason for this is quite clear: everyone wants the chops and leg. The head and hand and spring we could do without.

We have Large White boars and Landrace sows. This gives us the virility of the Large White and the finer body of the Landrace. The French Pietrain pig is often bred into this mixture. Again the aim with modern pigs is for leanness and high birth numbers. To be more traditional you can go for Gloucester Old Spots; these pink and black pigs have become popular again in recent years and they do produce excellent pork. They are also enthusiastic outdoor pigs so if you want to clear some land, they will thrive and look decorative at the same time. To get more ethnic still you can choose a Tamworth. These orange hairy pigs are an instant reminder of Tudor boar hunts; they are slow growers but if you are not in a hurry and are not aiming to make much money, it is interesting to have a go. Actually one way to make money from the more unusual breeds is to rear them to sell to other enthusiasts.

SELECTION

The selection of breed depends partly on how you intend to rear them and also on what you intend to do with the produce. If you are aiming for the home-freezer market, a good pork pig is necessary. Bacon pigs are generally produced on contract. We make our own bacon for home consumption — there are some recipes in Chapter 17. We make ours from mainly pork weight animals as that is what we produce most of. Having chosen a breed, or a hybrid, look in the magazines *Farmers Weekly* and *Pig Farmer*. These provide advertisements of suppliers. You can also look through the pig farmers in *Yellow Pages*. Many producers of pork or bacon pigs buy in all their stock as weaners — they never breed their own. Many breeders sell all the piglets they produce: they never grow any on except as replacement breeding stock. Some producers breed and rear — we do. One way to get in at the deep end is to buy in gilts. A gilt is a young female pig that is about to produce her first litter. You buy her, bring her home and then wait for the day. It should not be a case of 'buying a pig in a poke'. You can study the records of the gilt's parents and grandparents, the numbers of live births and so on. It is essential to go to a reputable breeder; here you will buy a good animal and get a lot of advice. If he sees you as a repeat buyer, you will get his full attention because top breeders make a lot of their income selling in pig gilts.

FARROWING

The gestation period of a pig is sixteen weeks. When you buy in a gilt you will be given an approximate due date. If you have had her served by your own boar then it is essential to keep clear records. It is all too easy to confuse pigs and their dates. To put the wrong sow into a crate would be to court disaster with the litter you have not protected. Put the sow into the crate a day or so before she is due to farrow. Give her plenty of short cut straw to lie on — long straw can tangle piglets. Many sows make a nest for themselves with the straw. When the piglets start to arrive you should take them away, wipe them clean and dry and pop them under an infra-red light until the total delivery is finished. The sow should not be allowed to eat the afterbirth or to lick the piglets if they still have blood on. This could overexcite her and tales of pigs eating their young are not old wives' tales. When all the piglets have arrived let them go to their mother. Most pigs make excellent mothers, they flop over on to their sides and give rhythmic grunts to stimulate the piglets.

Newly born piglets are wonderful creatures. They are quite ready to leap up and start exploring — they are inquisitive and full of 'go'. That is one of the main reasons why they get into trouble if allowed to do what they want to the instant they are born. Left to their own devices, they have an uncanny instinct of making straight for the sow's mouth — exactly where you do not want them until the whole situation has calmed down. A creep area that the mother cannot get into, complete with an infra-red light, gives them the greatest chance of survival. If there is only one warm spot in the pen and the sow can get to it, they will all pile into it and the little ones will get squashed. If you cannot obtain a farrowing crate or are totally opposed to using one, the next best thing is to fix a rail nine inches away from the wall and the same distance up from the floor; this at least gives the piglets some chance of escape. What it does not do is help anyone who has to assist at the birth. A heavy sow is not only a threat because of her size, she can bite with shattering power.

A sow will eat plenty of food once she has recovered from the birth and also consume a lot of water. If you are aiming to wean early, say at six weeks, you should put in some creep food with the piglets in the very first days. If you intend to wean at eight weeks then you can wait a little. Piglets must have an injection of iron in their first few days unless they are on open ground. When the piglets are born you must check their teeth; if they are extremely sharp, they must be clipped or they will damage the sow's nipples. In common with other lactating animals it is essential to keep an eye on the sow to check that she does not develop

Sow Accommodation

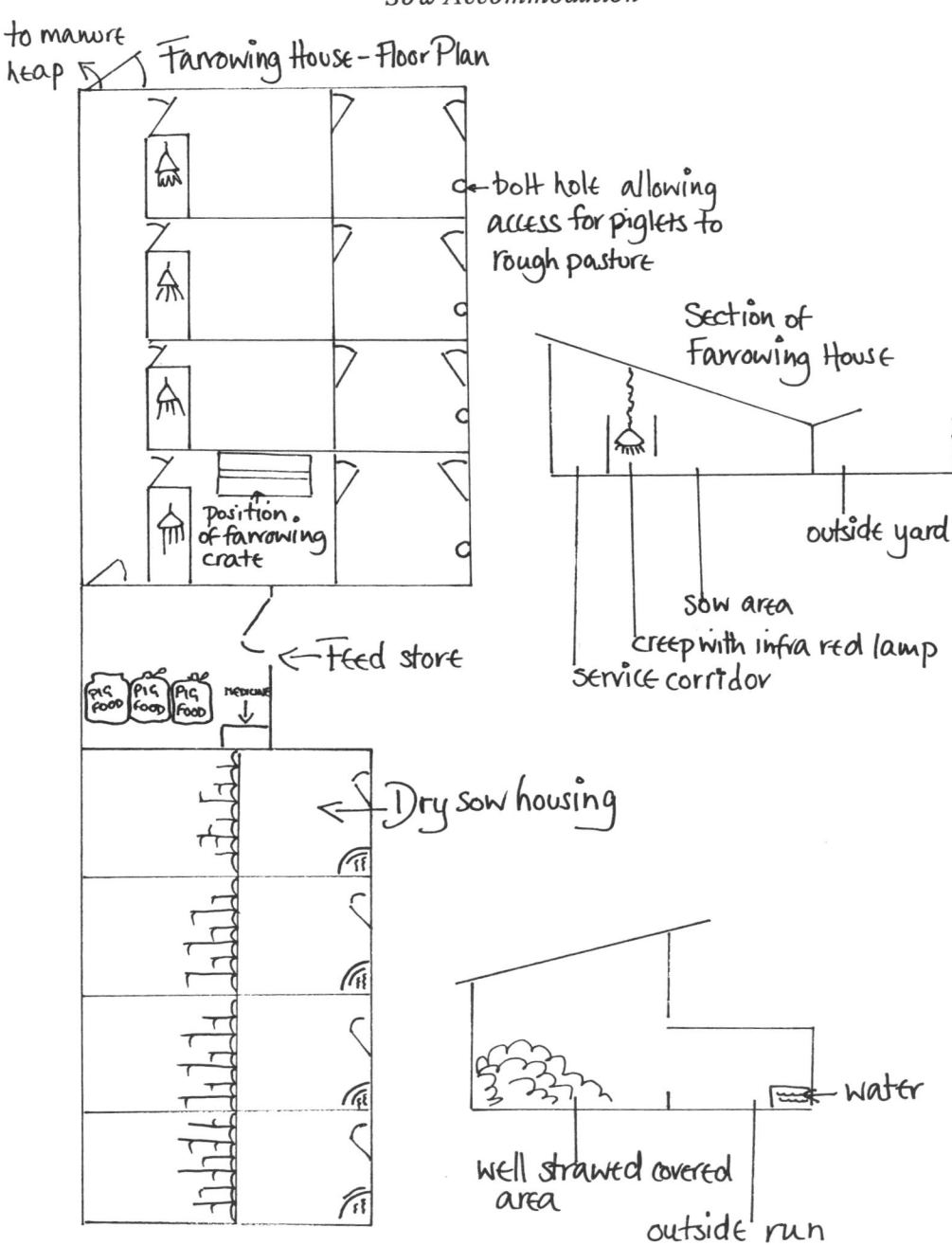

Farrowing House – Floor Plan

- to manure heap
- bolt hole allowing access for piglets to rough pasture
- position of farrowing crate
- Feed store
- PIG FOOD / PIG FOOD / PIG FOOD / MEDICINE
- Dry sow housing

Section of Farrowing House

- outside yard
- sow area
- creep with infra red lamp
- service corridor

- well strawed covered area
- water
- outside run

mastitis. If she does, the areas around the nipples become hard and painful to touch and naturally the piglets drop off in condition. The vet must be called immediately and if the condition perseveres, the piglets will have to be fed on a bottle. We never find piglets as amenable as lambs in this respect. They seem to feel that it is a great indignity to be handled in this way and very audibly make their feelings known. Of course, they soon get used to it.

When you are approaching weaning another fundamental decision has to be taken: whether or not to castrate. For years there has been a major argument between the meat trade and pig farmers. The meat trade is generally opposed to boar meat. However, if the pigs are slaughtered at pork weight, the animals are not sexually mature and there is no taint. The practise of castrating pigs is unpleasant to say the least. It is performed using an extremely sharp knife or razor. It is essential to know how to do it correctly and so if you intend to do it, ask the vet first. Or you can join us and many others who refuse to do it. Eventually it must be discontinued as it is an astonishingly barbaric practice.

When the piglets are eating the dry food well you can remove them to another pen and then you have a batch of weaners and a sow ready to begin her reproductive process again. If you do this at six weeks, you may well get two litters a year from your sow; if you leave it until eight weeks, you will get under two. When the piglets go off on their own, leave them for a few days on creep ration but then change over in a couple of days to a grower's ration.

RUNTS

Traditionally there is always a runt in the litter — in reality this is not always the case. Sometimes there are none and sometimes there are two. They are quite recognisable: they are smaller and weaker than their bullying brothers and sisters and tend to get trampled in the rush to the milk bar. If the litter is small, say eight or under, there will not be too much competition for teats and the weak one will probably cope. In higher numbers, it may well be pushed off all the teats, with obvious results unless you intervene. Runts will always grow a little more slowly than the others but we have always felt it was worth giving them a helping hand. They usually need encouragement to take milk from a bottle and sometimes the only way to get them started is to put a little milk into an empty syringe case (no needle) and very gently trickle it over the tongue. You must be very careful not to simply pour it down into its lungs or it will die but once it gets started on the idea it is off. If you cannot really face the prospect of all the fiddling then why not offer it around? The most surprising people will be tempted. The only awful price you have to pay for your act of mercy is that when the time finally comes and Grunter or Porky or whatever else he has been called is destined for the freezer, you find the whole family in a state of collapse at the thought. Of course, you cannot keep an ex-runt for breeding as it is inferior stock. This is one of the times when you wish you had never gone into pigs in the first place.

SOWS

Sows come into heat at three-week periods throughout the year, that is until they are successfully served by a boar. The sow will not come back into a heat after she has given birth until you wean the piglets. When they have been removed she will probably come into heat after two or three days but it may be as long as ten days.

BOARS

A mature boar is often a fierce creature. Even hybrids can have mediaeval faces with curling tusks and spiky hair. The problem with keeping a few sows is that you do not justify owning a boar and may find it difficult when you want your sows served. If there is a pig restriction movement in force it will be impossible. These movement restrictions are put into force during outbreaks of transmittable pig diseases and prevent the movement of livestock except to and from market. Many pig-keepers will not in any case wish to allow their boars to come in contact with sows from outside as there is a risk of infection. Having said this there are stud boars available in some areas; for some reason rural pub-keepers seem to be the likeliest owners. Presumably you can have a drink while your sow is being served. If you do decide to buy a boar, buy one from proven stock and follow any advice the breeder gives you. Not all boars know what they are about. We had a delightful boar named Fritz. His manners in the pen were impeccable, he obligingly moved around as you wanted him to, he dunged in a tiny corner and never slobbered when eating. Unfortunately, he was just too refined and we could never get him to be enthusiastic about his job. Sadly he had to go and a much more reprobate character filled his place. He, of course, was a great success even if he did continually try to eat your wellington boots when you cleaned out his pen.

PORK

This is the end of the production line. Pork pigs are ready at between 120-130 lb live weight. If you are aiming to sell the meat privately, take the pigs to the slaughter-house and collect them when they are ready. This will not be the same day as the pigs must be chilled. It is difficult to cut a pig that has not chilled sufficiently and if the slaughter-house is amenable, it is best to leave them in the chiller for two days. The slaughter-house will probably cut and wrap them if you want but much of your profit then goes in their charges. There is a cutting diagram for pork on page 146. You could always do as a friend of our did who enthusiastically bought a whole pig from us some years ago. Armed with a sharp knife and a saw, she reduced the whole carcass to six-inch-wide joints. As you can roast any piece of pork this was acceptable but not to her husband. He rebelled at being faced with continual nameless pieces. Now she buys them already jointed.

If you are producing bacon pigs, you must rear them to the weight your customer wants. There is a small market for suckling pigs which are totally milk-fed piglets. Most customers want them at about twenty pounds dead weight. It is sometimes difficult to get a slaughter-house to deal with them but the point to remember is that they are extremely likely to 'go off'. They must either be delivered immediately to the customer or deep-frozen. In any case, certainly avoid doing it in hot or humid weather. In other countries such as France and Italy, the pigs are killed and then processed into patés, pies, salamis and so on by the farmer. That is not done very much in Britain but we do process a fair proportion of our pigs that way. It is very useful to be able to process the head, collar, hand and spring and belly into patés and pies. Then you can sell the loin and legs at a very competitive price. There are suitable recipes for pork in Chapter 17.

Rabbits

Rabbits breed astonishingly quickly. Thirty to thirty-one days after a successful mating, up to ten of them arrive — minute, absolutely naked and blind. They proceed to grow at an astonishing rate. A hybrid, say a New Zealand White crossed with a Californian, may well reach two and a half kilos in eight weeks. This is killing weight. The traditional breeds such as Dutch, Giant Flemish, and so on will take about twice as long.

There has been a great increase in battery farming rabbits in recent times. Several large companies supply the equipment and stock; *Farmer's Weekly* carries their advertisements. The appeal has been to turn empty buildings into money-making enterprises. It is now clear that to succeed, these intensive units must be run with a great deal of skill and care. Highly bred rabbits tend to be highly strung and must be treated accordingly. Raising rabbits in wire cages requires very careful ventilation and possibly heating. Anything other than total commitment produces low returns per rabbit and as these ventures require a high initial capital outlay, they may not be successful. We keep our rabbits in a more traditional way using wooden huts. We get excellent returns and enjoy feeding and cleaning the rabbits. It is a personal occupation rather than an automated chore. Also, of course, as it is on a rather more gentle scale, we find our children and their friends are very happy to help. As well as selling Farm Gate it is worth calling on butchers and fish merchants. A regular supply of fresh rabbit may well sell. Freezer centres sell quantities of Chinese rabbit which has all been fattened in batteries: often the carcasses are minute. Most outlets like their rabbits skinned but some, notably fishmongers, like the skins left on.

BREEDING

A healthy buck can serve ten rabbits quite effectively. The doe should be well grown before she starts breeding, around eight to nine months. Take the doe to the buck's cage, not the other way round, as does fight intruders. Most bucks are keen and leaving them together for fifteen minutes should be sufficient. When the doe is pregnant she will require peace and quiet and gradually increasing food levels towards the end of her pregnancy. On the twenty-sixth day after mating, put a nesting box in with her. She will line this with hay and soft fur that she has pulled from her chest. When the doe has littered do not be tempted to disturb the youngsters; frightened does eat their young. If you leave them totally to her care for the first week they will soon be hopping about the hutch. It is better not to feed much greenstuff while the doe is lactating as it can have a laxative effect. The best way to provide water is in drip bottles. The water in them must be kept fresh. While the doe is lactating she will drink a great deal. If you usually use a bowl for water, you will need to put some mesh into it when there are youngsters in the cage or they will leap into it.

The young start to eat their mother's feed at an early stage so they will need some extra food if she is to keep in good condition. The young can leave the mother at six weeks. The doe will be ready to return to the buck in two weeks. The young stock should be reared on to killing weight which is about two and a half kilograms live weight. The easiest way to weigh a live rabbit is to put it in a string bag and hang the bag on a spring balance. If you give the rabbit anything solid to get a purchase on while it is being weighed, you are in for a struggle. If you have the time it is worth handling the rabbits and being friendly with them. It is then easier to handle them when you have to. It pays to take care with rabbits though because a scratch from them often turns septic and for some reason they often seem to scratch the inside of your wrists which is a tender spot.

Any stock required for future breeding should be segregated when the fatteners are ready. Does can be kept together, up to eight in a group if the space is big enough. Bucks must be reared separately from now on. Bucks will literally fight to the death. The whole cycle of mating, pregnancy, littering, fattening and breeding is very quick in the rabbit kingdom. When we built up to fifty breeding does, their offspring at various stages and the attendant bucks, we began to feel overrun. By using some simple mathematical progressions it was simple to see that if we increased much more, we or the rabbits would have to go! Although they are small compared to sheep and pigs, rabbits can fill freezers at an alarming rate. When we oversupplied our local market for fresh rabbit we started to make rabbit pies to sell to local pubs and restaurants. As long as the meat is well seasoned, rabbit pie is very good. We also make pâté with rabbit and a recipe is included on p. 156.

*Enchanting Wild Rabbits —
a potential source of disaster
for the rabbit breeder as
carriers of myxomatosis*

Hens

Probably the easiest of all livestock enterprises is keeping chickens for eggs. That does not mean that they require no attention at all, rather that chickens have fewer quirks than most other creatures. If fed and watered, kept away from hungry predators and given a little electric light, you can expect a modern hen to produce up to 300 eggs a year. 'Modern' hen implies a hybrid bird, specifically reared to produce a vast number of excellent eggs. It also implies that the hen is in her first laying year; in the second year, her yield will drop by 30 per cent.

The first step in deciding the basis of your chicken enterprise is to decide exactly what you want to market. The second is to find out how much you can sell. Eggs and table chicken are produced in vast quantities and competition for sales is fierce. Research in your area will prove if you have a potential market or not. Sales of eggs are mainly affected by price: if you undercut your competitors and still provide a regular supply of fresh eggs, you will be in business — for how long depends on whether you are still managing to make a profit. Price-undercutting can make egg production uneconomic; high fuel costs mean that delivery costs are a major factor. Free-range eggs have a limited market but they command a higher price. They are the subject of much argument today. Test-cases are being brought before courts of law all over the country. What exactly is 'free range'? Some producers claim that merely allowing access to a small area of outside ground to a large number of chickens is sufficient. Probably the only safe way to claim 'free range' is to have the hens roaming at will on your property and to let your customers see them. This means either selling Farm Gate or actually inviting the retailers to whom you sell to come and see the hens happy in their work.

Having established that you have a market for eggs and what the size of that market is, the quickest way to get into egg production is to buy 'point of lay' birds. These are advertised for sale in *Poultry World* and *Farmers Weekly*. A pullet sold as point of lay is generally around 18 weeks old. She will come into lay at around 21 weeks. If you do not wish to buy hybrid birds, you can choose a pure breed such as a Maran. You cannot expect as many eggs but you will get some extra entertainment. We have a Maran hen that is convinced she is a goose: she shuns her own kind and trots happily around on the end of the goose flock. Fortunately we do not have a pond!

Strange Sight in the Farmyard —
a broody hen will hatch fertile duck eggs

To keep up maximum egg production you must provide light for at least 14 hours a day. If your hens are totally restricted, you will need to supply all of it by electricity; if they are roaming about in the daylight, you only have to supplement this in the autumn and winter. If you are lazy (like us), you can have the light on a time-switch.

When the hens have finished their frantic nearly 300 egg stint they moult. Your beautiful happy hens look seedy, their combs shrink and fade and in general they look disreputable. They will come back into lay some eight weeks later and look normal once again. However, they will now only produce around 70 per cent of their first year's yield, so if you are aiming for the highest return per bird space you should get rid of them as they come into moult. In *Poultry World* there are always several advertisers requiring live hens. However, you will not get very much for your birds — probably less than a quarter of the price you paid for a point of lay. There are some better-paying ways to dispose of your stock. One is to advertise them locally as yearling hens and ask half the price of a point of lay bird — you will end up more in profit than if you sold for a quarter of the point of lay price and the newcomer will be satisfied with the lower yield for his lower outlay. Often, of course, these birds only sell in small batches so your involvement is higher. Usually you can also sell small batches of hens through the local livestock markets. The stipulation of sale in these markets is usually immediate slaughter but a surprising number of birds find their way to new homes. Another way to dispose of your hens is to kill and dress them and sell them as boiling fowl.

Obviously, if you have culled your laying flock, you must have another batch coinciding in egg production. Or if you are keeping your birds into another year, you will have to buy in eggs to keep your customers supplied. After all if you stop supplying, your customer will buy from your competitor and you will probably have lost out for good — an egg is an egg!

It is worth bearing in mind two last facts. One is that you can really only rely on your flock producing around 80 per cent of its capacity (and that is an overestimate if you are an egg-tray dropper); and the second is that selling to retailers has to be absolutely regular. The retailer will plan his stocking according to your delivery and he will not take at all kindly to sudden alterations, so apart from everything else you need a dependable vehicle.

HOUSING

Most egg production in Britain comes from battery hens. The birds are kept in small individual wire cages. Their food and drink arrive automatically and often the eggs are collected by a conveyor system. Owners of battery houses generally claim that their birds are healthy, cheerful and enjoy being fed without any effort and are happily producing a daily egg in return. Be that as it may, there is still a lot of strong feeling against keeping chickens this way and it appears that a return to earlier production methods which are more extensive would please a large sector of the public. Some battery houses have been converted to a system that is similar to systems that were widely used some ten to twenty years ago. Hens have free movement within an enclosed building, are kept on dry litter and are provided with food, water and electric light as needed. They can perch and lay their eggs in nesting-boxes. To make this system more extensive, access can be given via 'bolt holes' to a paddock outside the hut. This is often referred to as an aviary system. If there are two paddocks they can be used alternately. This lowers worm-transference and gives the birds access to fresh grass and insects. The next stage in extending the chickens' freedom is to remove the paddock wire and allow them 'free range'. You have to be quite careful with stocking rates as chickens can decimate an area if stocked too heavily. If you have several hen-houses and want to free range, you must position them some distance apart so that the birds develop their own territories and do not all return to one house at night. Free-range birds definitely require more looking after – if you want to keep your flock intact you must check that none are left out at night and that all the 'bolt holes' are closed. Creatures other than chickens can use them! There are time-clock and light-sensitive systems that will close the holes but of course they do not count the chickens.

If you have quite a lot of land and abundant labour, you can have yet another system. A hen-house of 50 birds on an acre will glean what it can without affecting other crops – a 10-acre field could carry 500 hens as a bonus crop. However, as that field will no doubt carry a fox, stoat, rat and mink population, quite a lot of ingenuity is required to outwit them. Obviously electric light is out with this system so you have to use storm-lights or an equivalent.

There is also a mobile system of housing. Today it is most often seen as a backyard chicken-run but it used to be practised extensively and may well yet return on a wider scale. Here the hen-house is on wheels. It has a run attached which is also portable. The whole structure is moved its own length once a day giving the birds access to fresh ground. This way the birds are protected from predators (at least four-legged ones), and still enjoy fresh grass, bugs and so on.

Chicken Fold — ideal for paddock or orchard use.
The floor of the run is open to allow the birds to forage in captivity. The whole construction should be moved regularly.

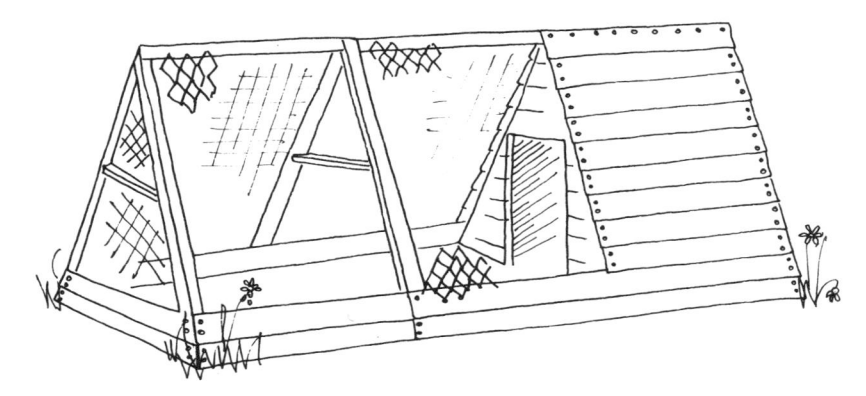

Clearly, there is a wide range of ways to keep your chickens. Many garden hens live in converted sheds with fixed runs. As long as the runs are kept fairly dry, the birds happily scratch about and produce a few eggs. The eggs are delightful to look at and quite delicious, but this is not really money-making.
Warning: do not be tempted to free range chickens in a small garden. They will move your flower-beds on to the lawns and garden paths will disappear. They are very busy little creatures.

FEEDING

On any scale of poultry-keeping other than the very smallest, it is simplest to buy in a prepared feed from a corn merchant. Hens will certainly relish household scraps, boiled first to stop ant disease transference, but it takes a large family to keep even half a dozen layers going. Layers mash is formulated to supply your hens' complete diet. Today calcium is generally included but it is worth checking on this. If it is not included, you will need to supply some oyster-shell; just a couple of handfuls lasts a dozen birds for ages. If the birds did not receive this extra calcium, they would need to consume 12 lb of grain each to produce one egg! No calcium, no eggs. Chickens also require a supply of grit. If they are free-range, they will collect their own. If they are not, you will have to supply it. Without grit, they cannot digest what they eat. No grit, no eggs. Allow 4 oz layers mash per bird per day and then a little extra. As a 25 per cent reduction in food intake causes a 50 per cent reduction in egg production it is clearly worth feeding your workers well enough. Fresh water should always be freely available.

Hens love some whole grain sprinkled about to scratch for and if you want to entice them into their building, they will follow a trail of grain — at eating pace, of course. Our hens roam about devouring weeds with gusto; one of their favourites is a many-seed-carrying plant known locally as 'fat hen' — presumably its name reflects its popularity with domestic fowl over past centuries. The hens also mow the grass. Giving hens greenstuff means that their eggs will have deep-yellow yolks; if your chickens cannot collect their own greenstuff, take some to them. Tie it up for them to reach up to so that they do not foul it.

EGGS

Collect the eggs at least once a day and more often if you can. Your hens will obligingly lay them in nesting-boxes where they are fairly safe but the safest place of all is in the box on your customer's shelf. If you are producing an appreciable number of eggs for sale, you must contact your local Ministry of Agriculture and Fisheries. Egg producers are numbered for identification and checked on regularly. Your eggs must be washed and measured and sold in batches of a similar size. All this is to protect the consumer which is quite right. It seems a shame, however, that this standardisation has brought the sale of a box of eggs into the same position as the sale of a package of detergent. If you have a market for Farm Gate sales, you can get away from the branded image. Then your customers can have a more personal purchase, you can have a higher profit and everyone is happier.

Packaging Your Eggs Attractively

'FARMGATE' PICKLED EGGS

free range eggs in spiced malt vinegar

10 oz
283g

TABLE CHICKENS

Producing table chickens is another mass operation today. Vast flocks are raised to some 6 to 8 weeks as broilers. They are killed, plucked, gutted and frozen almost as quickly as those famous peas. Herein lies the key to your possible success in this market. Why do fresh farm chickens taste far better than frozen mass-produced ones? Part of the secret is that traditionally, after a chicken has been killed and plucked, it is hung in a cool place for some 24 hours before eviscerating. Birds prepared in this way taste of chicken. If you can reach a market that appreciates this, your success is assured. Again, Farm Gate sales are excellent. It is astonishing how far people will travel to buy direct from the producer. Sunday afternoons can be very hectic if you become established in a suitable area for 'runs in the country'. If you are close to large centres of population, you will find it pays to advertise in local papers, shop windows and so on. 'Word of mouth' can also work dramatically. A few years ago our bank manager bought half a pig from us: the next thing we knew we were inundated with orders from the rest of his branch — a good product can sometimes sell itself.

It is important to aim for repeat business. To sell one chicken to a customer is only the start; you want his business on a regular basis. After all, a regular buyer of your chickens will naturally ask you for turkey and other larger fowl.

Selling to butchers and other retailers puts your business into another legal setting. In this case you must be a registered producer. You are required to comply with certain regulations concerning separate killing- and producing-rooms, running water, drainage and so on. The Ministry of Agriculture and Fisheries has further information on this. There are many changes still being effected in the regulations due to our membership of the EEC. In this market you may well be forced to consider deep-freezing your chickens: many retailers only sell frozen chicken. Of course, you will lose your higher price for fresh birds but it may mean that you can do fewer deliveries. The problems associated with selling frozen chicken are very similar to those associated with selling eggs into retail outlets — image and price. The giant producers have standardised the product so much that it is generally the 'known brand' that sells or a much cheaper product.

REARING PROGRAMME

The simplest way to start producing table chicken is to buy day-old chicks. You can find different varieties for sale in *Poultry World* and *Farmers Weekly*. Select a producer, 'phone your order, send a cheque and then turn up at the railway station on the appointed day to collect your chicks. A word of warning about collecting birds this way. Some years ago we collected several boxes of quails. They were segregated into breeding trios, one cock and two hens per box. Beautifully packaged in their little cardboard houses, they proved too much of a temptation. Just a quick look into one box resulted in a dapper cock doing an amazing imitation of a helicopter. He rose quite vertically, wings whirring, and then did circuits and bumps round the inside of the car — fortunately all the windows were closed! Of course, little chicks cannot manage the same kind of escape but it is probably a wise rule to keep everything intact until you are right beside the brooder.

A brooder is basically an artificial mother hen. It has a heat source which in sophisticated models is thermostatically controlled. If you are using an infra-red bulb, you just raise it or lower it to alter the temperature. A large lampshade covers all the chicks; from the edge of this a skirt hangs all the way round almost touching the ground. A barrier of some kind, often cardboard, is put a little distance outside the skirt to keep the chicks in. The gap under the skirt allows for ventilation. The brooder should be kept at an even temperature. If you run the brooder for a couple of days before the chicks arrive, the temperature will be constant. Chicks are extremely susceptible to infection. The brooder itself must be scrupulously clean. If you use the same room regularly as a brooder room, it must be totally disinfected between batches. You need 50 sq. ft per 100 chicks in a brooder and 7 sq. in of hover space per chick. A ring of netting close round the hover restrains the chicks for the first few days; it can be removed after Day 4 to allow them the full brooder space.

Decrease the temperature gradually. If you have 10 ft of snow around you then you will need to keep the heat going. During the summer, you may well be able to dispense totally with the heat after four weeks. If you have bought hybrid birds and have kept them growing well, they may well be up to weight at eight weeks. If you have a profitable market for poussin (birds of around 1 lb in weight), they may be ready at four weeks. Obviously, it is not worth feeding your birds to reach higher weights unless you have a market for them.

A grower's ration mixed to a paste can be fed throughout the fattening time. When the chicks are small they find it easiest to eat from little lumps of food on flat boards. As they grow you can progress to more economical feeders. As with all livestock enterprises, the aim is to get the food into the intended animal, not all over the floor! Chicken feeders should be designed to prevent the chickens from soiling the food. The simplest and possibly most effective design for this is a roller suspended a few inches above the trough. When the chicken tries to perch on it — as it will — it does a spectacular forward roll. It will not do a repeat performance. If the bar is fixed, it simply sits there dropping chicken manure into the food which it then no longer feels like eating. From eating absolutely minute amounts, the birds progress quite rapidly to eating about 3 oz each per day. To allow the birds to grow more slowly and hopefully produce a tastier chicken, let them have access to the land. A mother hen takes her brood on walkabouts from a very early age and you can see them happily pecking about; they are simply animated balls of fluff at this stage but do manage to survive a vast number of hazards under Mother's watchful eye. Fattening chickens raised in an incubator have no mother hen, so you have to perform a similar function. They need guarding from four-legged predators such as rats, crows and mink. When they are very small they even require protection from cats.

The French have a subsidy system that encourages feeding maize to poultry. This produces a beautiful, yellow-coloured chicken. If you can be sure of a suitable market, such as expensive restaurants, it is worth producing slow-maturing, full-flavoured chicken. Without this market, the only person for whom it is worth producing an extra-succulent bird is yourself. Of course, if you throw a party to consume this delicious bird, you may establish a market after all — your guests! There is an excellent chicken recipe shown in the illustration on p. 151.

MULTIPLYING CHICKENS

So far we have assumed that all the chicks, layers and fatteners, are being bought in. You may well decide to breed and rear your own. In fact, the margin in cash terms of buying or home-rearing point of lay birds always seems very small. However, home-reared birds have a bonus — they are often the most economic and prolific egg-layers. After all they have not had a traumatic move and a change of routine to adapt to; they are not faced with a whole new lot of bugs to contend with either. The same argument applies to chicks for fattening. Naturally it is only worth breeding from really good stock of a suitable breed. A chicken that naturally produces only a few eggs a year — take as an extreme example the jungle fowl which only lays one clutch of around a dozen in a year — is not going to produce an economic 300 eggs however much you feed her.

To produce fertile eggs cockerels are required. With a few hens, you need one cock to 8 to 12 hens. If you are running batches of

100 hens together, one cock to every 15 to 17 hens is sufficient. Hens in their second year tend to lay fewer but larger eggs. These eggs often hatch better than first-year ones. If you select the best-looking of your first-year hens, keep them until they have finished moulting and then run the cocks with them, you should get an excellent result. The eggs will be fully fertile five days after the first mating; eggs laid will continue to be fertile for five days after the cocks have been removed. Fertile eggs can be hatched under a broody hen or in an incubator. You can tell a broody hen by its unwillingness to leave the nest: if you lift her up she will trot back again in a few minutes. She can hatch up to a dozen eggs quite happily. She will sit on them for 21 days.

You can take the chicks away at this point if you like and launch into a rearing programme or you can allow mother hen to be the brooder. Feed her well with some extra for the chicks and watch them grow. Mother hen is an excellent creature who will happily hatch goose and duck eggs for you too. Hybrid birds do not go broody very often — it was bred out of them as it interferes with egg production. If you want to use broody hens then keep some of the pure breeds such as Marans of Sussex. You can also hatch the eggs in an incubator — this is how most eggs are hatched commercially. In vast modern hatcheries you hardly ever catch sight of a chick. Instead of the operation being carried out by a jovial farmer it is run by white-coated technicians, all in the interests of hygiene. That is well worth remembering if you buy chicks from a large hatchery, as they will have been brought into the world well away from dust and creepy crawlies and are very susceptible to infection to start with, so on with the white coat! There are many different sizes of incubator, from one-egg up to thousands in capacity. The one-egg size is apparently a gimmick but does work. Some incubators have plastic lids to let you watch the action. It is worth getting an incubator with a quick turning device. The eggs must be turned at least twice a day to stop the embryos sticking to the shell membrane. This must be done for the first 18 days. With a turning device it is no hardship to do it four times daily; if you do it by hand you may suffer from boredom but, more importantly, all that touching with your warm hands may upset the temperature in the incubator. Hold the eggs up to a testing lamp between the fifth and eighth day and then again between the fourteenth and eighteenth. In the first case the healthy eggs will contain small dark spots radiating blood vessels and in the second healthy embryos will fill the shell well. Discard any dead ones. After the eighteenth day the incubator should remain closed. Incubators differ in design so follow the manufacturer's instructions carefully throughout and then wait for the big day. The chicks do not require any food for the first 24 to 36 hours of their life and should be kept in the warming drawer of the incubator until the hatch is complete. From now on the chicks enter your rearing programme unless you intend to sell them as day olds. If you are growing the chicks for point of lay, you can fatten the cockerels as table birds. Although there is a market for stock cockerels it is far smaller than that for laying birds so you will inevitably have to kill some for sale or, of course, your own consumption.

Ducks

Duck-keeping is often inspired by pond ownership. Any area of water is enhanced by a few ducks floating on it. If this is your motivation for going into duck-keeping, it is worth bearing three important facts in mind.

Ducks on a Pond — their wings should be clipped or they may well leave in late winter

1. Duck eggs can transmit dysentery and other illnesses — still water is a great source of tummy bugs. If you intend to eat or sell the eggs, make sure that the pond is continuously being filled and emptied. Or better still keep the ducks off the water.
2. If you intend to eat or sell for eating fat ducks, again keep them

off the water. Exercising in water leads to tough ducks.

3. Baby ducklings do not always float and mother ducks seem to be unaware of this fact. Again keep them off the pond. In fact, ducks are not nature's most careful mothers and duck eggs are really safest brought off under a broody hen. Of course, she will not have the slightest inclination to take them off for an instant bath. Having said all that against the pond, there are a couple of reasons why you should allow ducks on to it. One reason is that the heavier breeds of duck often find it difficult to mate unless they are on the water. Therefore, when you want your eggs fertilised, let the birds mate on the water, collect the eggs and incubate them artificially or under a broody. The second reason is that ducks really do love water so if all you want to do is improve your view then let them on to it. Ornamental birds can have free access to water if you are breeding them. Mandarin ducks and other ornamental waterfowl sell very well if they are in prime condition and swimming around certainly keeps them sleek and colourful.

DUCKS FOR EGGS

Ducks do not lay eggs in nesting-boxes like the obliging chicken. In fact, they will drop them anywhere. It is therefore advisable to leave the ducks in their night quarters until well into the morning: that way you have a lot fewer eggs to hunt for.

Khaki Campbell ducks are the best variety for egg-laying. They are lightweight brown-coloured birds that lay up to 300 eggs a year. A duck does not need artificial light as a hen does and the eggs are larger than a hen's. However, ducks do eat one and a half times as much as a laying hen, about 6 oz of layers mash a day. If you allow the ducks to run on your vegetable garden, you will find that they are great devourers of slugs and unlike the enthusiastic hen, will not enjoy your vegetables as well. Ducks start to lay when they are four or five months old and are always much more expensive to buy than a laying chicken, often up to three times as much. *Farmers Weekly* and *Poultry World* carry advertisements of suppliers.

Duck eggs are something of a specialist market; health shops will often provide an outlet and local agricultural markets often provide custom. People who like duck eggs will often travel to buy them so it is worth persevering to find a market. It is worth pointing out to prospective customers that duck eggs make superlative sponges. Perhaps it is also worth bearing in mind that one of the authors of this book spent a week in an isolation hospital having picked up something evil from a duck egg. We hasten to point out that the egg in question was not one of our own; our policy now is only to eat those we produce ourselves and never to eat one soft-boiled.

DUCKS FOR MEAT

Almost all the ducks we eat are Aylesburys. The Aylesbury is the traditional white duck with orange bill and feet. A good Aylesbury will lay up to 100 eggs a year so this breed is sometimes referred to as dual-purpose. However, if you work out the comparative cost of producing an egg from an Aylesbury or a Campbell (three times as much) it is quite obvious that Aylesburys should be bred to fatten. Fed well, an Aylesbury can grow to around 8 lb live weight in 8 weeks. This is when the birds should be marketed. It is the easiest time to pluck them as they are moulting and not yet in full adult plumage. Ducks are not nearly so easy as chickens to pluck.

In France the Rouen duck is the most widely eaten. It is a handsome, black and white bird which takes some six months to reach the weight of a two-month Aylesbury. This slower growth is said to give more flavour. The bird is generally killed by smothering. This is said to add to its particularly fine flavour; what it certainly does is make it more likely to 'go off' as it has not been bled. It has to be cooked within a very short time of killing to be safe and for this reason it is banned from sale in the USA.

HOUSING

Ducks remain on the ground so their housing can be quite simple. What is important is to have a floor that is easy to clean so that the eggs do not become contaminated. The housing must be fox-proof — the nursery rhymes are all quite true: foxes *love* ducks and geese. There should be at least 2 to 3 sq. ft of space for each duck and that is assuming that these are only night quarters; if your ducks are also confined during the day, they must have a lot more space.

Aylesbury Ducks — the traditional white farmyard birds

It is easier to maintain them in flocks of less than 50. Ducks are timid creatures and should always be treated with care or they will frighten themselves into going off lay or, when they are small, they will stampede into the corners and trample the little ones. We always whistle when approaching ducklings: if they have heard your approach from afar, they seem quite happy. You can use their reaction of darting away in a bunch to move them about. Raise your left arm behind them and they move to the right and vice versa. It is not quite as effective as moving geese in this manner but certainly more effective than moving hens. If you try to move hens like this, you will generally find that they frantically cluck and dart off in several different directions; it is simpler to resort to bribery and lay a trail of grain to wherever you want them to go. (As a last resort it is worth remembering that chickens roost in the dark and if one or more of yours goes missing, creep around shining a torch up into neighbouring trees. This process is extremely amusing to watch but often very satisfactory and much better than letting a runaway fall prey to a four-footed predator.)

The best way to feed ducks is on a similar ration to hens but in a sloppy mash. They are very wasteful feeders and we always let some chickens in with them to clear up — waste not, want not! If you feed the ducks whole grain, feed it in a shallow trough of water. They like fresh water to drink and if they can get into the water container they will swim in it. If the ducks are allowed to forage they may well obtain enough grit and greenstuff; if they are confined, you have to supply at least the grit. Ducks that are allowed to roam are happy creatures; you will only be as happy if you clip their wings, otherwise someone else will probably get a gift from the skies — your ducks!

MULTIPLYING DUCKS

1. Run ducks and drakes together: four to five ducks to one drake. If you have a heavier breed, let them run on water.

2. Collect the fertile eggs.

3. Hatch them in an incubator or under a broody hen. Of course, you can let nature do her best and allow the duck to sit on them. The number of ducklings reared will almost certainly be far less.

4. When hatched keep them warm, if not with a duck or hen then with an infra-red lamp and a cardboard surround. Leave them in this for at least two weeks depending on the outside temperature. The infra-red lamp should be gradually raised as the ducklings grow. It is simple to see if the lamp is at the right height: too low and the ducklings rush away as far as they can from the heat, too high and they crowd together underneath the lamp.

5. Rear growing ducklings on a grower's mash: five times a day at first, three times a day at eight weeks, thereafter twice daily. Feed as much as they will clear up within half an hour.

6. At around eight weeks, take all the meat birds and dispose of them. Laying birds are grown on until they come into lay at around four months. These you either use for breeding or egg-laying or sell as point of lay.

DUCK BREEDS

Peking ducks are more upright than Aylesburys but similar in colouring. The Pekin duck is slower-growing but eventually larger than the Aylesbury. It will lay up to 130 eggs a year. Whalesbury ducks are a cross between an Aylesbury and a Welsh Harlequin. (The Welsh Harlequin is itself a cross between Campbell ducks.) It grows well and lays about 200 eggs a year. A Muscovy is an odd-looking bird with red wattles. When it is mature, the flesh is very strong-tasting. The Nantes duck is smaller than the Rouen duck and is much prized by the French.

The best way to sell ornamental birds is through local papers where you can reach other pond-owners.

ORNAMENTAL DUCKS

There are all sorts of ornamental ducks such as Mandarins and Carolinas.

DUCK FEATHERS

Fully feathered ducks will yield up to one-fifth of a pound of feathers per bird. If you have a few pounds of feathers to sell, put them in a polythene bag with a few holes punched in, tie a pretty label round the neck of the bag and take them to a local craft shop. Patchwork cushion-makers are often good customers for fine feathers. This is assuming that the feathers are clean; if it has been raining for days, you will have to keep the ducks in the dry for a couple of days before you kill them, otherwise the feathers will be muddy and damp. Not only will the feathers be messy, it is also much more difficult to pluck a wet bird. If you have large amounts of feathers it may well be worth advertising for direct sales. As well as craft-users requiring feathers for pillow and duvet fillings, there is a growing interest in making feather flowers. The feathers are often dyed for this and the white feathers from an Aylesbury are ideal. Traditionally, the curl at the end of the drake's tail was used as a superfine paint-brush.

14

Geese

Geese can be very friendly creatures yet some geese are ferocious. If yours are of the latter variety, your main problem is to keep clear of them. If not, your problem comes at Christmas when they may be destined for the table. If you have had geese happily chortling around the house for several months, the silence when they disappear is horrible. However, if that is what they were bought for in the first place — to fatten and sell — you must steel yourself and make someone's Christmas special by providing an excellent goose. Be warned, geese are the worst birds to pluck. It really takes three pluckings: the first for the feathers, the next for the down and the last to remove the little quills, forerunners of further feathers. A badly plucked goose is reminiscent of a hedgehog and will probably put off a first-time goose-eater for the rest of his life.

Geese can be kept for profit in several ways:

1. For table eating, traditionally at Christmas (Thanksgiving fare is also goose). Goose used to be eaten at Michaelmas but this is not often celebrated today. There is movement afoot to encourage the use of goose as a celebration bird throughout the year.

2. For egg sales, either to owners of incubators or broody hens or to egg-painters — the egg is blown empty and then painted and decorated.

3. For breeding, to provide goslings for sale.

4. For selling as pets. Geese are very effective orchard-mowers and watchdogs; you are instantly aware of intruders when the geese set

up a clamour and very often they frighten off the unwanted visitors (of course, sometimes they frighten off the welcome ones as well!).

Goslings are often advertised for sale in *Farmers Weekly* and *Poultry World*. You can sometimes buy grown geese through local newspaper advertisements. If you put a gander to every two or three females, your eggs stand a good chance of being fertile. Geese tend to 'do their own thing' if at all possible. They will wander as far as they can on your property and, if allowed to, will potter off on to your neighbours. They will remain inside sheep-netting and similar boundaries if you have clipped their wings. If you have not and they are given a little encouragement then quite literally the sky is the limit! You must bring them in at night or your Christmas dinner will be the fox's dinner instead. All those cartoons about foxes drooling with longing for a succulent goose are absolutely true. Two-legged predators also favour geese. Geese are valuable birds and if you are not very careful about keeping them secure at night, particularly when they are plucked and ready to leave, you may well wind up as one of the growing number of victims of rustlers.

When you want to bring your geese in from ranging, just walk behind them. When you want them to go right, you hold out your left arm; if you want them to go left, you hold out your right arm. Yes, you do look quite funny doing it, however it is most effective.

GOOSE EGGS

Most geese lay in the spring. A good female may lay 40 to 60 eggs. Chinese geese lay throughout the year and will lay at least 60, if not more. With a lot of care this may yield 25 goslings but the emphasis is on the word 'may'. Goose eggs are difficult. Fertility is a problem and geese themselves rarely make good mothers. Of course, you can eat the eggs or sell them to someone else to eat. They are just like a hen's egg apart from their stupendous size. Small children literally shriek with delight when presented with one fried. If you buy the jumbo egg-cups that are sometimes available, breakfast will never be the same again. If you do intend to hatch the eggs, either use an incubator or a broody hen. Mother goose may well manage to raise some of her young but you will have to accept that the numbers reared will be low and you may have a complete disaster. We have had goslings squashed by their overprotective parents and a goose will not protect its young from rats although a hen will. Having said all that, the sight of a happy family of geese with goslings in tow is delightful. This sight of a happy mother hen with goslings in tow is funny and delightful. The sight of an incubator is neither; it does, however, make the best producer. The care of the goslings once they are hatched in the incubator is similar to the care of ducklings (see pp. 116-17).

The great increase in the popularity of egg-painting as a hobby or indeed as a business has lead to an increase in the price of goose eggs. If you find a good outlet for your eggs into this market, it is possibly worth selling all your eggs this way. Each egg sold to a painter could fetch £1: this means that one laying goose is bringing you £40 to £60 per annum. If you manage to hatch 25 of the eggs and sell the goslings for £2, that is £50 income. Mathematicians among you are no doubt already clamouring that the remaining 15 to 35 not hatched could still be sold to the affluent egg-painter. This would make a total of between £65 and £85. But if you have tried to incubate these eggs, they may well be in a state of yuck inside their shells and if you have ever tried to blow a 'gone-off' egg then you will appreciate that the egg-painter will not be very happy, to say the least of it.

FATTENING

The theory about fattening geese is simple. Goslings hatched in the spring go on to the growing grass and can then fatten on grass alone up to the end of September. When grain was gathered less effectively than today, the geese were set on to the gleanings in the fields where they finished beautifully in time for Michaelmas. Geese ready at this time of year are known as 'green geese' and they are the most tender. If you want the geese to go on to Christmas in good condition, you will have to start supplementing their food. A grain mash will be eaten with enthusiasm and we add boiled potatoes which they love. If you aim to feed so that it is eaten up within half an hour, feed them twice a day and always have plenty of fresh water available. In Russia where vast flocks of geese are raised, they are kept confined to concrete yards. This is so that the concrete can be easily washed down; geese leave very messy droppings. If you keep them in an enclosed space you will have to fight a continual battle against the amount of droppings they deposit. The geese that are intended for the table should reach between 10 and 14 lb plucked dead weight. Any geese that you are keeping to breed from should simply be kept in good condition. They should certainly not be underfed but neither should they put on too much weight.

The Goose and One of its Uses

A Goose Quill Pen

Above — slit
Side — cut under
Prime flight feather

at its happiest grazing — the domestic goose.

The Goose Breeders Association has recently been formed; it is connected with the Duck Association and it will be interesting to see how the promotion of goose compares with the enormous strides that duck has made into the poultry industry. The success of goose would not be a new affair, rather a comeback. Elizabeth I was apparently enjoying roast goose at Michaelmas when she was informed of England's victory in the Armada. Full of enthusiasm (and possibly wine), she decreed that goose should be eaten on that date for evermore. Goose-breeders would like this custom revived. It is being forecast that beef and goose will take over from the turkey as traditional Christmas fare. As turkey is now eaten widely throughout the year and large joints of beef and goose are not, they obviously have speciality value. The other line of argument is presumably that people are more prepared to buy expensive cuts of beef and expensive goose at the festive season. For this forecast to work, someone has to produce more geese!

GOOSE BYPRODUCTS

Goose feathers are used for stuffing pillows, cushions and duvets. In the USA, live plucking is practised. The geese are plucked several times a year and the value of the bird comes from the feathers. Apparently, the meat is considered to be of negligible value.

Prime wing-feathers can make quills, excellent for improving handwriting. Well-cut quills can be sold to craft outlets. (There are instructions on how to cut quills in the figure on p. 122).

If you choose to further process your goose by cooking it, you are left with another useful byproduct — goose grease. This grease has the lowest melting point of all the poultry greases. It is soft and oily with excellent waterproofing powers. A little rubbed on a dog's paws or a horse's hooves will prevent chaffing in the snow. Goose grease rubbed into dry and cracking leather restores it magically; the leather can then be washed with saddle soap and polished. Finally, goose fat makes the most delicious sauté potatoes in the world.

MAIN BREEDS

1. The Embden. This is the largest and probably the most widely available. A full-grown gander can weigh 14 kg and a goose can weigh 9 kg. It is white with an orange bill, legs and feet. If you want geese that the children will recognise from all the storybooks, this is the breed to have.

2. The Toulouse. This has a grey head and some grey in the plumage. The gander grows to 12 kg and the goose to 9 kg. This is the poor goose that was force-fed to produce fat livers for pâté de foie gras. Now that the market for this kind of pâté is declining, the practice of force-feeding has also declined.

3. Brecon Buff. This is similar in colouring to the Toulouse but has a pink bill, legs and feet. The gander grows to 9 kg and the goose to 7 kg.

4. The Chinese. This looks like an extra-large duck. It is usually brown or white and weighs up to 7 kg for a gander, 6 kg for a goose.

5. The Roman. This is similar in weight to the Chinese.

15

Dairying

It is accepted in the farming community that to be in dairying you have to be totally committed. You have to be prepared to employ specialist labour or to be totally involved early in the morning and on into the evening for seven days a week. To be successful at producing a peak amount of milk from any animal requires a high degree of stockmanship in the person who milks and feeds the animal. High standards of cleanliness are required so that the milk produced is wholesome. There need to be suitable buildings and if necessary suitable items of equipment to process the milk. All that being said, to come in close contact with and to milk animals is one of the most satisfying areas of livestock enterprise.

Some years ago there would have been little point in sticking to the word 'animal' when talking about dairying. It could have been safely assumed that the animal in question was a cow. But in the past few years there has been a great renewed interest in milking goats and there is now an upsurge in the popularity of milk sheep. To start off in a dairying enterprise is simple: you just buy a lactating animal. The forethought necessary to avoid pans of spoiling milk and an unprofitable venture is considerable. The first decision has to be what type of animal you intend to milk.

GOATS

The easiest animal to start with is a goat. This is for several reasons, the first and most obvious being the price. You can probably buy eight or more good goats for the price of a good cow. There are, of course, extremes of price in any market, but a normal healthy goat (one that does not have an inflated price tag from exotic breeding) is a cheap animal. The foodstuffs necessary to produce gallons of milk from your goat are often simpler to obtain than the foodstuff required by a cow. In the summer at least, a lucky goat provided with lots of branches and brambles, some decent grass and a little concentrate will thrive. The goat's favourite food is generally that despised by other grazers. The expression on the faces of our goats when they are allowed access to a new patch of brambles or a piece of hawthorn hedge hitherto denied is one of sheer bliss. Of course, if you are blessed with prolific grass, the goats may seem a little more difficult to please. They will eat some grass but it is not their natural favourite and if your grazing is too soft, you will have to go out collecting some scrub for them or at the very least give them some hay. Not all greenery is safe for the all-consuming goat. Rhododendron makes them extremely ill and yew poisons them. Many textbooks claim that rhododendron is an instant poison but we had a mass escape of seven goats and they consumed quantities of it and the result was not death. It was the vilest green vomiting imaginable which came up with astounding force from the sad goats. It lasted for two days and then they all recovered. Rhododendron was certainly a strong poison to goats but it was not lethal.

Another good thing about goats is their size. When you try to move a full-grown dairy cow you realise that it is an immovable object. In fact, instead of moving away from you the cow usually leans right back into you and you are the one who moves. A goat will certainly react to a shove, usually with a deer-like bound. Goats also take up a lot less space than cows in housing and milking facilities.

When you want to sell goat's milk, your choice is not the same as with the cow. There is no Milk Marketing Board to buy goat's milk in bulk although in a very few areas there are co-operatives. Usually you have to sell the milk yourself. In some areas the recent interest in goat's milk has meant that producers have swamped the market. To be economical it is generally reckoned that you must receive one and a half times the going rate for a pint of cow's milk. In our area at present you are fortunate to achieve the same as cow's milk. The answer here if you want a viable proposition is to process the milk into cheese or yoghurt.

The Goat

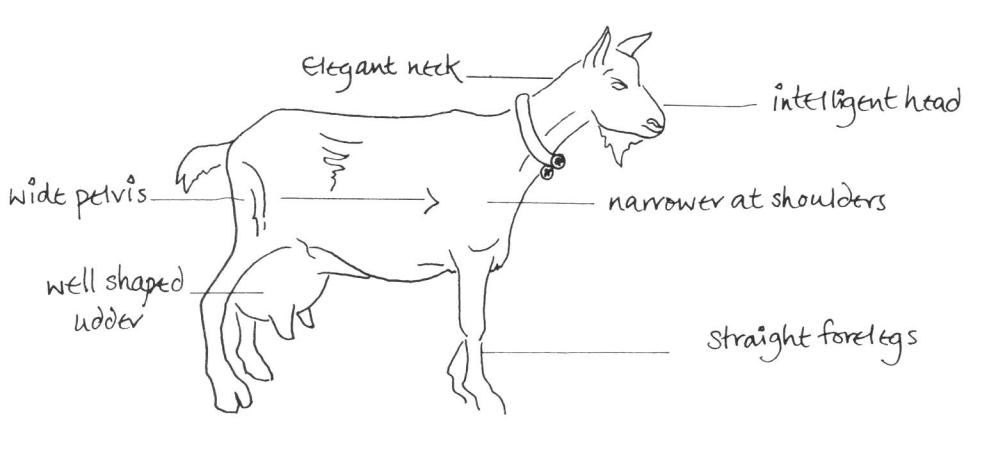

Handwritten labels on goat diagram:
- Elegant neck
- intelligent head
- wide pelvis
- narrower at shoulders
- well shaped udder
- straight forelegs

The above is a 'near perfect' goat. Some incredibly ugly ones still give an excellent milk yield.

The final major point to consider when comparing goats and cows is that you do not need a licence to sell goat's milk whereas you do need one to sell cow's milk. This is not simply a question of being involved in health checks and hygiene standards, anyone in milk production should be able to stand up to those. The point is that it is difficult to obtain a licence to sell cow's milk unless you have an established dairy. If you have to start from scratch, the type of building required can cost a great deal to build. You can safely handle the smaller quantities of goat's milk, on the other hand, in a kitchen or utility room.

Goat's milk is essential to some allergy-sufferers. Our son had colic as a tiny baby; eventually he was put on to goat's milk and the improvement was tremendous. Similar cases of allergy are always cropping up and much of our production goes to allergy-sufferers. The only point to remember if you intend to base an enterprise on such a market is that the sufferers quite often recover. A customer who was buying a pint a day suddenly disappears, possibly not to be replaced.

One way to simplify the sale of goat's milk is to freeze it. Goat's milk freezes well. (Cow's milk can be frozen but it will separate on thawing.) Another way to use goat's milk is to make cheese. This is not always easy — goat's milk soft cheeses tend to weep after some hours. The sight of a pool of liquid around the nicest little cream cheese is enough to put off most buyers. You can put the cheese into little plastic pots that will contain the liquid but the only real answer is to take extreme care in the manufacture of the cheese.

There are various breeds of goat available in Britain. The one from the story-books, large and white with a bell round its neck, is the Saanan. These are usually docile but extremely strong when they decide to pull. They also seem to us to be the most independent breed, at least all the Saanans we have had have been determined to lead life at their own pace. They are the breed that produces the most milk. To get the richest but generally smallest yield, you can go for a strange-looking creature called a Nubian; its splendid broken nose and long, lapping ears also mark it out as an individual. For some reason these seem the most aristocratic of goats and they tend to take a while to decide if you are friend or foe. The Toggenbergs and Alpine goats are delightful creatures to look at. The first are brown in colour, the second black. They have little tassels hanging from their necks and delicate features. The most difficult goat we ever had was a cross between a Nubian and a Toggenberg. The cross was not our idea. We were asked to take the goat as we were goat-enthusiasts. We did not at the time realise it was an act of mercy to the original goat-owner. We called her Jubilee and expected her to settle down after a little while; she never did, she just got worse. If you tried to lead her on a rope she managed to turn in the minutest circles until you gave up entirely. She escaped from absolutely anywhere. Finally and most infuriatingly, whenever you did manage to milk this awkward creature she managed by extreme contortions to drink the milk you had painstakingly obtained! Presumably she is still annoying someone somewhere, unless of course someone gave up entirely and had her turned into kebabs. We passed her on, hopefully to a more patient home than ours.

SHEEP

Much of what has been said about goats can be applied to keeping sheep for milk — with one important difference. If you offer a milk-producing sheep hawthorn and brambles to eat, she will not appreciate it one bit. The heaviest yielders are lowland sheep and they like their traditional diet of rich lush grass. We have milked Jacobs as well as the more usual Friesland. The Jacobs managed to assume an astonished expression at the indignity but when they got used to the idea they enjoyed the extra feeding it gave them. With any animal, milk yields increase according to feed levels until you reach that particular animal's peak. It is no use pumping pounds of expensive concentrate into a goat that will physically only ever produce a couple of pints at each milking; a really good animal may well give you a gallon but that is dependent on your feeding her so that she can make the most of her genetic make-up. A sheep gives less milk than a goat and to be profitable you should aim for at least twice the return for cow's milk.

Very little sheep's milk is sold in liquid form although it is apparently more easily digested than goat's or cow's milk. Ewe's milk makes delicious cheese — blue like the delicious Roquefort or white and fresh. It has a specific acid flavour. It also makes delicious yoghurt but we like to drain this and make another type of soft cheese (see page 168). Specialist cheeses can sell through delicatessens and health shops but the vital factor to take into consideration is the appearance of the cheese after a few days. Like goat's milk soft cheeses, it may tend to weep. As with goat's milk cheese, the only way to avoid this is to be very careful about how you make it.

COWS

The cow, once you have decided to cope with her bulk, is a very nice creature. At least almost all of them are. If you do come across an awkward dairy cow, it may be a nervous heifer that has just dropped her first calf. If she should kick you when you milk her, you can at least afford her some sympathy. She has a long milking life ahead of her. If the cow is an established kicker you either have to become adept at avoiding her or get rid of her. The whole point about dealing with cows is that you do not argue with them. They are too heavy.

You can choose the type of cow for the enterprise you have in mind. Choosing one of the Channel Island breeds is quite traditional for an enterprise with only a few animals. Although their yields are lower, the fat content is higher — you get extra per pint. They are also less wear on the land as they are light and, of course, they eat less than the bigger breeds. They tend to prefer milder climates so if you live in a cold and windy spot you may have to keep them in for a fair part of the year or even consider putting rugs on them. The milk from the Guernsey is a really deep yellow, the cream rises beautifully. We find the whole milk too rich and only use skimmed milk in tea and coffee. The cream is fantastic for making butter although if you compare the cost of the butter you make to the butter you buy, you will head straight back to the supermarket. This is because the butter we buy is made from subsidised milk. It is therefore most profitable to sell the milk or cream and buy your butter. We confess to enjoying our own home-made stuff.

If you aim to make cream by skimming it off the top of milk that has stood for a while, do go for a Channel Island cow. At least until you become very skilled at it. You can see clearly the difference in colour where you have not collected all of the cream. A really skilled skimmer will leave the surface of skimmed milk totally free from grease. You can sell the cream in tubs labelled 'Channel Island Cream'. You cannot say double cream unless you have used a machine to take the cream and you can be certain that the fat level is sufficient. If you use a cream separator, it must work efficiently or you will not get all of the cream. You can regulate machines to produce different grades of cream. Unfortunately these useful gadgets are expensive. Almost everyone who buys a small one wishes instantly that they had bought a bigger size. The hand-operated ones tend to wear more quickly than the motor-driven ones. Even if you can buy a second-hand one you are likely to find it expensive. Of course, cream can be clotted. We produce most of our cream this way. (There are details on pages 135-6). Again if you want to use this method it helps if the cream is a dark colour.

Butter and Cream Equipment

Electric butter churn

Stainless steel Milk churn

Butter hands

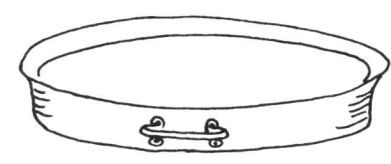

a broad pan for making Clotted Cream

friend in the Granary
enemy in the Dairy

The Ayrshire produces ideal milk for making a really good cheese. The fat globules are evenly distributed through the milk and therefore stay in the cheese more easily. To produce bulk milk, the traditional high yielder is the Friesian. Every farm in children's books has fields populated with contented black-and-white high yielders. They are big cows and their feet are also big. If your land tends to get waterlogged, beware of heavy cows.

OFFSPRING

All milk animals require good feeding, regular worming and to be made pregnant regularly to keep the milk cycle going. For the sheep this is easy. Most sheep-owners have a ram or at least access to one from a neighbour. Goats are slightly more complex. You may have to travel some distance to find the billy you want. Not many goat-owners keep billys. To start with many goat-owners only have one or two animals. Apart from that, a male goat really stinks. No doubt that will incense someone whose billy smells delightful. However, all the billys we or our friends have come across smell, at least for most of the year.

To get a cow in calf involves one of two happenings. Either you have or have access to a bull, or you contact the AI man. The AI man is someone from the Milk Marketing Board who will come and artificially inseminate your cow. This gives you a great choice of father. All the bulls are specially selected for performance. You can choose the breed you want, either the same as the cow or another breed, to produce a specific type of calf. If you intend to produce more milkers of your own, you will probably want to breed true to type. In that case your heifers will grow up and go into your herd. Often, as in the case of Channel Island calves, the males are not valuable as they do not grow to a heavy beef carcass. You must either sell them for a low price or fatten them yourself. We have fattened Jersey bull calves ourselves. They must be neutered at an early age as Channel Island bulls are very unpredictable and can be vicious. The meat is excellent and the fat a yellow colour. The market in general does not like the lightweight carcass but if you intend to consume it or sell it yourself, it is certainly worth trying. To produce heavier carcasses from a

Channel Island dam, you can select a bull from a breed such as the Dorset. This produces a good beef carcass. From Friesians and other larger cows you can produce all sorts of beef animals. A pure Friesian bull calf grows very well although many farmers prefer to cross with a sire such as a Hereford. It is worth keeping very good records of the sires you select and the results of your progeny. All livestock enterprises can benefit from records. It is easy to see where animals grew slowly, which dams produced heavy milking heifers and so on.

All dairy enterprises necessarily produce youngstock. Whether you keep them or sell them depends on how you intend to run the enterprise. With limited space, it is probably worth selling all the youngstock and simply buying in replacements as needed. With plenty of space, the attraction in raising your own youngsters is obvious.

MILKING

Many producers milk goats and sheep by hand; very few milk cows by hand. The smaller animals are quicker to milk and often their owners enjoy the peaceful routine of hand-milking. This is compared to the noisier use of machinery and the necessity to clean the machine out afterwards. It's easier with your hands — you just wash them! The peaceful routine of hand-milking in fact only comes after some days or weeks of agony. If you have never hand-milked and launch straight in, the exquisite agony of pains in your tendons and muscles cannot be described. Your grip on the teat should be as soft as silk, your squeeze gentle but the regular stresses on unprepared muscle makes the milker, not the milked, a creature of torn nerve ends. We started off our own venture with goats milking by hand because in those early days manufacturers of milking machines thought the goat market too small to bother with. With the boom in goats came the machines and truthfully we very thankfully joined the ranks of the automated. We have only milked cows by hand when absolutely necessary, for example, milking the odd house cow when our elderly machine started having hiccups. They were always perfectly happy, as we smiled and spoke softly in their presence. If you are milking a cow by hand you must be fairly quick about the whole operation. The cow 'lets down', that is releases her milk, for only about seven minutes. That sounds a lot until you are faced with a heavy yielding cow and then it's like 'beat the clock'. The different pulses required to milk cows, goats and sheep are now all catered for by the machinery experts. (We are reliably informed that they also cater for llamas and camels should that interest you.)

The obvious increase in yield when a dairy cow goes out on to fresh grass may become a thing of the past. Hydroponic grass units — there are some churning out tons of sprouted grass daily — could make it Summer all year long. This makes it theoretically possible for dairy cows never to set foot on grass at all. If you cut all the grass they consume from the field and cart it to them you can also become an indoor milk producer. The thought that those gentle beasts never eat a single daisy or tread on a little ant in the production of that great foodstuff seems to remove a lot of the pleasure from drinking it. However, when the rain is pouring and your precious land is being chewed up by great bovine hooves, the question can be seen in quite a different light.

IN THE DAIRY

The milk you take from goat, sheep or cow will either be in a pail if you milk by hand, or in a churn of some type if you milk by machine. If you have a large number of animals, there is another possibility: it may flow straight from the animal to a bulk tank. With a bulk tank, your system will incorporate filters and a cooling system. If you do not have this degree of automation, you will still have to filter and cool the milk. With the milk from one goat you can simply strain it through some filter paper and put it in jugs or bottles in the fridge. It is more effective to cool even a small quantity of milk by standing it in a receptacle in a bowl of running water. With larger amounts of milk, the system becomes more complicated. With a few cows you can strain the milk from one churn to another through specific milk filters. There are water-cooled radiators to run the milk over to cool it or you can develop Heath-Robinson-type gadgets. The aim is the same however you do it: to strain the milk of unwanted dust and impurities and to cool it in order to slow the natural processes of 'going off'. The problem with handling milk is that it is an extremely perishable product. It will also pick up flavours from the air, for example, silage clamps too close to the dairy can taint the milk. Odd greenstuff consumed by the milk animals can also produce 'off' flavours. The usual example quoted to illustrate this kind of disaster is the flavour produced in cows milk when the herd has happily consumed quantities of wild garlic. The traditional remedy in cases like this is to make the garlic-flavoured milk into soft cheese. Of course, if you had intended to sell the milk whole or as fruit yoghurt, your problems are clear.

EEC regulations are aimed to prevent the sale of untreated milk. The threat of these regulations being enforced across the board seems to have been lifted at least for a time. Many people appreciate the flavour of 'raw' milk and farmers who bottle direct are naturally fighting this threat to their way of life. There is now a relatively small milk pasteurisation unit on the market which may make the possibly inevitable compulsory pasteurisation more feasible on the farm. If you intend to sell your milk to the Milk Marketing Board, you will be kept informed as to the levels of antibiotics and dirt in your milk. The obvious position should be that there is none. If the milk is sold direct by you or further processed, there are few tests unless you are processing cow's milk. If you produce milk that is not absolutely clean and then process it into cheese you will find that odd flavours and moulds develop. It is worth establishing a clear routine for dealing with the milk you produce. There are small churns available should you wish to keep your own milk in churns or if you find that regular customers would like to collect their milk like this. Just to carry fresh milk in a small churn seems to take you back to a slower age. At the other end of the scale you may wish to put your milk into heavy-duty polythene bags. There are specially printed ones available for goat's milk and they certainly make freezing very easy.

Cream pots can be bought in difference sizes and with special printing on them such as 'Channel Island Cream'. Clotted cream can be sold in small tubs as well or in big square boxes if you are selling to a retailer who wishes to break it down from his cold counter. As Kent is not traditionally a county producing clotted cream we have had little competition when selling ours. The flavour of farmhouse clotted cream is nowadays fast disappearing. Most clotted cream is manufactured in bulk from cream that has already been mechanically separated. Traditionally the milk is put into large flat pans, the cream is left overnight to rise and in the morning the whole pan is very slowly heated until the thick flakes of clotted cream form on the surface. The pan is then cooled and the cream removed using a skimmer. If you do not have sufficient space to process all the cream you want, you can produce more cream per pan. This way you must first separate the cream and then run it on to a little milk in the bottom of the pan. It will clot the cream but there will not be as much crust. We find that we produce the most delicious clotted cream using Guernsey milk.

Cream Tea

Yoghurt is now very popular. You can make fruit ones, either buying a specific fruit mix or using your own home-made jams. You can make yoghurt from whole or skimmed milk. The latter is always popular with slimmers, but the former has the better flavour. If you want to be really greedy, try making yoghurt using evaporated milk. The flavour is phenomenal! Soft junkets and other creamy sweets can certainly make a profit if they are fed to paying guests or, if your property is suitable, you could consider serving lunches, coffees and cream teas. For a capable cook the margins achieved in this kind of venture are excellent. To find outlets for this kind of dairy produce it may be possible to come to an arrangement with the owner of a pub or restaurant. Although the proprietors of such places may not have the time to be involved in such a venture, they may be willing to allow you to use their facilities for a moderate fee.

Taking dairy work into cheese-making is following the tradition of our ancestors who were endeavouring to save some of the summer overproduce in a nutritious form for consumption in the winter. The very simplest way to produce a soft cheese is to leave milk to sour and then strain it. This generally produces a sharp-tasting soft cheese. You can beat in a little cream to make it softer or salt or herbs to flavour it; it is also delicious with soft fruit and it can, of course, be used in cooking. All the other forms of cheese are based on the same principles. You do something to encourage the milk to separate into curds and whey. This can be done simply by leaving the milk to sour quickly in a warm place or using a cheese rennet to coagulate the milk. Then strain the curds off and process them as you wish. You are always left with whey. If the curds have been efficiently made and processed there will not be much whey left. Some whey, however, contains solids and butterfat. In any case, the whey is nutritious and easy to digest. Years ago some farmhouses fermented the whey and produced a sparkling drink from it. We use it a lot in baking, it makes excellent scones. You can further process the whey to remove all the solids and make another type of cheese. Or you can use it in another valuable way: feed it to poultry for the finest birds imaginable. Any cat or dog thinks they are pampered beyond belief when fed on it and pigs guzzle it.

This kind of lower level use is not good enough for skimmed milk, that is milk from which you have removed the cream. Although in some cream-producing farms it is still fed to the pigs, and this use is encouraged by government subsidies, it is really better used for human consumption. Anyone on a diet appreciates the lower calories in skimmed milk (compared with whole milk), and anyone with a history of heart problems would benefit from its lower cholestrol levels. For your own consumption you may prefer to use it in place of whole milk, particularly if the cows you have are Channel Island.

Goat's milk makes excellent cream and butter if you persevere for long enough. Some goats do produce quite creamy milk although sometimes waiting for the butter to turn is a lengthy process. To go all the way and produce hard cheeses is one of the most satisfying dairy enterprises as long as things go well. If they do not, it is one of the most disappointing.

Hand-churned Butter

There are many regional cheeses that have disappeared from our tables due to the centralisation of cheese manufacture. However, it seems that we are beginning to revive old recipes and be more inventive in the dairy. Although we are now competing with the continentals in producing a Brie-type of cheese in Britain, it is not suitable for producing in a non-specialist environment. This type of cheese requires an extremely controlled environment to mature successfully. It also requires very specialist knowledge and techniques. Similar-shaped cheeses, large round flat ones, can be produced satisfactorily using limited equipment and techniques but the consistency of the cheese is not the same. Small Stiltons sell well at Christmas and you may wish to produce similar-sized cheese of a different variety for marketing at that time. Your product may require local advertising and possibly even tasting sessions — but it would be extremely nice if the traditional upsurge in the cheese market at Christmas benefited our own cheese industry as much as it does the French.

The Kitchen

The possibilities of production using domestic appliances — a food-mixer, a cooker and a fridge — are considerable. To change home-produced soft fruit into jams and chutneys takes you into a different market and means, of course, that your product has a longer shelf life. To change pork into pies and cheese into cheesecakes opens other areas. Prepared foods can be sold into several markets. The very simplest to cater for is the direct public. The public can be fed in your home (a bed-and-breakfast type of venture), or you can take the food to them (catering for weddings and so on). These ventures are often catered for entirely from a domestic kitchen. If you intend to produce goods for sale into the retail trade, you will legally have to produce in a totally different kitchen from the one in which you cater for the family. In theory this applies to making cakes for sale from the 'farm gate' and other similar produce. In practice, very few people comply with this. Within a small radius of our own enterprise there are several houses displaying boards advertising not only vegetables and eggs for sale but also obviously home-produced cakes.

Let us start with the concept of actually feeding people in your own home. This is often one of the biggest percentage profits in the food production area. People in a large number of areas can obtain passing guests using the Tourist Board lists. It is often worth asking local pubs and hotels if they have any overflow to pass them on to you. If you can provide a comfortable bedroom, and if possible a separate bathroom, the venture can be simplicity itself. You can put together home-produced eggs, fried potatoes and bacon to produce a breakfast your visitors will remember. If you also produce home-baked bread, home-made marmalade and jam, you will probably wind up with repeat business from your clients and their friends. To make the enterprise more profitable, offer evening meals as well. A well cooked meal based on home produce is economical for you and delicious for your guests. If your house has an unused granny annexe or something similar, you could take in self-catering guests. This is the most sought-after holiday accommodation today. Then you can offer vegetables, possibly home-produced eggs and meat to your guests. All these 'guests' are of course of the 'paying' variety. Even if the area you live in may not seem instantly recognisable as a tourist area there are other kinds of business to attract. People travel for business and to see family. If you advertise, you may well tap a market that will bring in much repeat business.

To cater for functions requires a different style of cooking. The arrangement of food is all-important. You may also find that it is necessary to provide dishes and plates. We have provided this kind of food for several people who did not feel able to produce the kind of food required but wanted to do the rest of the venture. This meant that they advertised for the business, made the arrangements and organised any china and cutlery needed and staff as required. They ordered the food they required from us and collected it on the way to the event. This kind of sharing of responsibility can work very well in allowing people of different talents to make use of one market. It is always essential to remember that for the people for whom you are catering this is a very special event. When you are producing the fourth dressed turkey and sixth veal and ham pie on a hectic pre-Christmas Saturday this is easy to forget. It is always worth aiming for repeat business. Families that have weddings also have christenings, businesses that celebrate Christmas one year will do it again the next. If you have produced a really good table and the party was a success, the repeat business will be yours. The biggest annoyance to many people employing caterers is when they see that you have overcatered for the event. Although nobody wants to run out of food, it is always horrifying to see great quantities of food being removed after the event. Although the customer will already know what he is paying, this clear evidence of waste loses many people repeat business. If you are new at catering for numbers, you may find that this is your biggest headache. If you cannot stand the thought of undercatering then at least keep your back-up supplies out of sight. The customer will appreciate if you explain that you always have an emergency back-up in case of ravenous appetites. He will not appreciate seeing two half-carved turkeys being removed when one clearly would have done.

The Fruits of Effort

To produce food for sale into pubs and other similar organisations is another type of enterprise. The publican's prime concern will be portion-control. You have to live with that concept at the front of your mind to succeed. Very often pies and casseroles are dished up by bar staff. Unless the portions are clearly identifiable, the public gets an extra-large helping and the publican gets an extra-low profit. Items such as large apple pies rarely get ordered more than once — a few slices from the pie one day and the same the next. By the third day the apples are possibly fermenting, the pastry has gone soggy and more profit goes into the dustbin. The aim in all products for this market has to be good presentation coupled with awareness of the market you are in. Many publicans are very happy to explain their needs to you. They will often persevere to reach an acceptable end-product. This is dependent on you making quite clear at the outset that you are prepared and able to be flexible. Meanwhile, of course, you must keep a very close eye on your own profit margins. To start with you should work out a minimum order. This is the amount of business you require on each call to justify the trip. When supplying fresh food your deliveries will have to be close together. If you intend to supply frozen food, you will have to transport it so that it does not start to thaw in transit. For small orders and small distances a frozen food box is satisfactory. If you have to carry some of the delivery around for a whole day it is not.

To sell into the retail trade is the most challenging aspect of food production. Here your product is scrutinised by shoppers, shopkeepers and health control officials. The product, its packaging and shelf life must all stand rigorous tests. The Belgian pâté that sits in the cold counter of any grocer's will remain stable for weeks if kept trimmed. Although the manufacturers point out that the product should be sold quickly the shopkeeper knows that it will last should it not sell well. A pâté made without the factory facilities, the antiseptic forms of manufacture and preservatives, will certainly age most unpleasantly. The products you offer must be able to survive worse treatment than you would give them at home in your own kitchen. All packaging and labelling must conform to current EEC rulings. There are all kinds of different instructions being effected and discussed and unless you wish to fall foul of officialdom, you have to keep up. Manufacturers of various goods have to be registered. If you aim to produce for the retail trade then it is worth seeing your local standards officer before you commit yourself to expensive packaging. One of the traps that newcomers to this type of cooking are often tempted into is to try and produce a product that is identical to a competitor's. A factory-made product will look different. Anyway part of the appeal of your product to the consumer is often that they are buying something special. Some 'dairy' fudge contains additives that are bought commercially in vast bulk. It is this that gives commercial fudge a specific appearance. Without the additives your fudge will look different. It will look like 'old-fashioned' fudge. Fortunately, that is sold for a higher price than the commercial kind anyway. But if the market you approach says it wants the first type, you must gracefully decline unless you intend to set up a confectionery factory.

The Buffet Table

Kitchen Recipes

PORK

To Use Belly of Pork in Quantities

Rillettes

If you sell jointed pork, you will almost inevitably be left with excess belly. The simplest way to convert this into a higher priced item to sell into a different market is to make rillettes. This is a kind of potted pork sold widely in France. We sell ours to delicatessens and specialist food shops. Properly made, it keeps extremely well which makes it a better proposition than pâté for the shopkeeper.

The amount of rillettes you can make depends on the amount of belly available and the size of your cooking facilities. If you intend to cook them on top of the stove, you will need heavy-bottomed pans as the cooking is a slow lengthy process. We use the oven, with lidded dishes. Then the cooking, which takes around four hours, goes on without invading the whole work area.

Method

1. Take the skin from the belly. This is quite easy as long as your knife is sharp. (You can use the skin for something else.) Cut the belly into pieces about one inch square. If the belly is really fatty — this is all the meat you need; if it is quite lean, add extra fat — trimmings from the whole carcass are ideal.

2. Put all the meat into dishes and add about a ladlefull of water for every three pounds of pork. Cook slowly so that the fat just

Cutting Pork

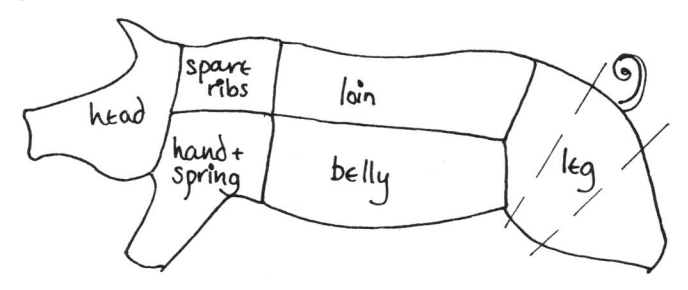

A pork weight pig is cut as above. The leg will provide three good joints. Every bit of the pig can produce crackling — the secret is to do nothing at all to the skin and roast it at 400°F.

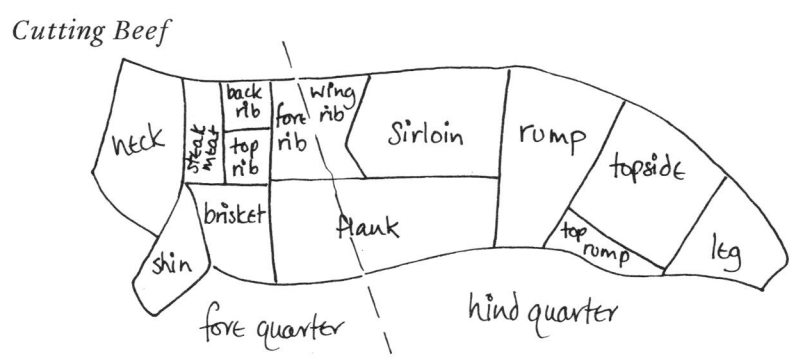

Cutting Beef

Cutting a whole beef carcass is a marathon job. It is possible to have it butchered into 'prime joints' at the slaughterhouse to make handling easier.

Cutting Lamb

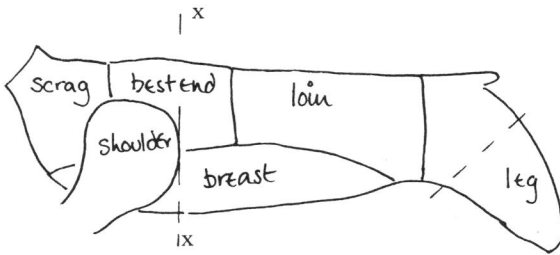

— for a very light weight lamb cutting along x — x provides an excellent roasting joint. A heavy carcass should be totally jointed as above. The leg and shoulder can be divided into two.

simmers slightly for four hours. You can remove some of the fat as you go or you can leave it in. Stir occasionally so that it does not stick.

3. At the end of the cooking time have some fine sieves ready over bowls big enough to contain the fat. Strain the hot meat and fat through the sieves. Take the meat and put it into a shallow bowl; pull it apart with forks. If you have a food-processor, you can speed this up by dropping the meat on to the revolving blade. But be careful not to overprocess it and never mince it or you will not achieve the required texture for rillettes.

4. Mix a little of the strained fat into the meat and season well with salt and pepper and other spices such as cloves and ginger. Pack the mixture into sterilised jars. Pour over a good layer of strained fat to cover.

5. When the pots are cold the tops can be covered with aluminium foil. You can put a decorative paper printed cover on this for presentation. If carefully made, these pots will last for six months in a cool place. Any extra lard produced can be packaged in waxed cartons for sale.

To Use Head of Pork

Many purchasers of half-pigs would rather not have the head. If you can offer an alternative, such as a few packs of lard, you will get over one of the objections freezer-owners have to buying complete sides. Faced with several heads to process, you can make brawn if you wish. The problem with selling brawn is that you are competing with a low-priced, mass-market product. An excellent product to produce is a small cheese-shaped round of a rillette-type consistency. For serving fresh it can be rolled in very finely chopped parsley. If you wish to keep it for some days in a refrigerator, paint it with extra lard.

Method

1. The method is quite simple. The heads can be brined or not to start with. Give them a scrub in tepid water to make sure that they are really clean. Put the heads in the oven — two or three halves will stand up side by side in a large baking-dish. Cover the whole

thing tightly with aluminium foil. Allow the heads to cook very slowly. (Slow-cooking operations are very simple if you have an Aga or something similar. With other cookers it is just a question of selecting a temperature that a quantity of fat simply simmers at. Not a boil, a much gentler action.) You may need to add a little water during cooking if insufficient juices are formed to keep the bottom of the pan from burning. Usually, particularly with brined pork, the water is not necessary.

2. After four or five hours of cooking, the meat should be falling from the bones. Allow the heads to cool and then pull all the meat, skin and bits from them. Anything that looks appetising is now put into a food-processor or chopped finely by hand. You could add parsley now but it means that the little pâtés will not keep for more than a day. Process the whole lot until there are no recognisable lumps. Then mix in a little extra fat from the baking tin.

3. Line a pudding bowl with muslin and put in dollops of the mixture. About one pound of pâté makes a good size for presentation. Tie the muslin firmly, take the bundle out of the bowl and shape it effectively to look like a tiny Gouda. Put this in the fridge to set.

4. When it is quite chilled remove the muslin and finish shaping with a knife. A well designed label can be stuck on the centre and the whole thing wrapped in clingfilm. It is a very nice product to sell to pubs and restaurants. A slice with toast makes an unusual and delicious hors d'oeuvre.

To Use Hand and Springs of Pork

Having disposed of the head, made rillettes of the belly and sold those ever-in-demand joints — legs and loins — you may well end up with the hand and spring. Many pig farmers eat this joint in preference to any other. The meat has the sweetest flavour. The public very rarely agree. The awkward carving necessary is often the deciding factor. The simplest way to sell this pork is to cut off all the meat, cut it into small pieces and sell it as casserole pork. It is becoming more accepted that pork can make a delicious casserole and these ready-cut cubes find a good market. The next stage is to take all the trimmings from the carcass with any extra fat and turn it all into sausage-meat. To have a good texture it is worth adding one-third of the pork weight in fresh breadcrumbs. The kind of seasoning you use is very much up to personal taste. We like to add grated lemon peel to our sausage-meat and to season well with black pepper. Sage is a very traditional herb to use. You can concoct special barbeque sausages by adding paprika and pork-rind. Try adding wholegrain mustard. The sausage-meat can be sold as it is or made up into sausages. Or you can use some of the sausage-meat in raised pies. We sell a variety of pies to pubs and restaurants. They are not the same as the mass-produced ones but they do slice well, have a good flavour and they do not have great lumps of pastry at each end. The basic method of production is similar; the different flavours come from the various ingredients used. The decoration on top of the pieces is used to enable quick identification. For example, the pork pie has a pig shape on it in pastry and the chicken pie a bird. Here is a recipe for making a raised pie using sausage-meat.

Raised Pie

Method
1. Having produced a well flavoured sausage-meat, mix in a fresh egg and a tablespoon of flour to every pound. This gives a good slicing pie. The traditional long slicing pie is made in a long loaf tin about twelve inches in length. For this size pie you will require two pounds of sausage-meat and another pound or two of pre-cooked chopped meat. Use one pound if you are producing a pie to be sold at the pub bar. Customers do not want a piece of pie that may fall apart and be difficult to eat balanced on a lap. To cater for a restaurant or function where the food is eaten at a table use two pounds of chopped meat. The chopped meat can be of various types — a mixture of chicken and ham is delicious as is well-seasoned rabbit. It is a good idea to vary the flavour of the sausage-meat you use with the different fillings. A sage-flavoured red sausage-meat goes well with ham, a lemon-flavoured one with game.

2. Now the meat is prepared you can make the pastry. The best-flavoured pastry for this kind of pie is hot water crust. It has the finest flavour if you use home-produced lard. You will need about

two pounds of pastry for each large pie. To make the pastry, put one and a half pounds of flour into a warm mixing bowl. Mix in a heaped teaspoonful of salt. Put six ounces of lard into a pan with twelve ounces of water. Bring this to the boil and pour it into the flour. The trick now is to put on clean rubber gloves. To get the best pastry you knead away until the mass looks like alabaster. As you can imagine, this is very daunting with bare hands! Even wearing rubber gloves you will have to remove your hands every few minutes; however, the result will be a good workable paste. Far better than that produced using a spoon or in a machine. Put a warm tea-towel over the pastry while you grease the tins. Do this well as the grease in the tins helps to brown the outside of the pastry. These pies can be made in oval moulds with hinged sides. However, if you are making pies in bulk, the whole process can become chaotic; it is much easier to use the oblong tins. In fact if you are selling to a customer who wishes to slice the pies before sale you will find that they do not appreciate the wastage they get at either end of the oval pies. The ovals are very impressive on a buffet table though: one or two can be arranged with oblongs providing the bulk.

3. Take two-thirds of the pastry and drop it into the pan. It should be cool enough to work like plasticine; if it is too soft, wait a little while. The aim is to work the pastry when it is stiff enough to hold its position up the sides of the tin but soft enough to manipulate. Working from the middle of the pastry, force it up the sides until it overlaps slightly all the way round. Then go back and work in the corners if you are using oblong tins. Any thick bits that are left will look unsightly in the finished pie; the corners and ends require special attention. Keep the remainder of the pastry covered while you work. With practice this process is simple and you will find that you can judge the correct thickness easily.

4. Put one-third of the prepared sausage-meat into the bottom of the pie, again making sure that it goes right into the ends and into the corners. Customers do not like being served a slice of pastry when they ordered pie. Now layer in half the chopped meat. Layer it lightly, when the pie is finished you will fill it with well flavoured jelly and there need to be spaces for it to run between the pieces of meat. Put on another layer of sausage-meat, another of chopped

meat and then finally sausage-meat. The meat should now be domed up in the middle: the next bit of pastry will take the shape of this sausage layer.

Granny Anstey's Devonshire Chicken

> **Granny Anstey's Devonshire Chicken**
>
> Take a fine table chicken
> 2 sweet apples - cored + chopped
> 1 large onion - peeled + sliced
> 2 oz butter, ½ pt white wine
> ¼ pt thick cream
> parsley
>
> **Method**
> Lay the dressed bird on apples + onions in deep casserole dish. Dot with butter, pour wine over, cover + cook for 2 hrs at 350°F. Remove bird to heated serving dish. Add cream to casserole contents + boil rapidly to reduce + thicken. Pour over chicken, scatter with parsley & serve.
> Good eating!

5. Take the remainder of the pastry, roll it out on a floured cloth and then invert it over the pie. This does save the tearing of pastry that often happens with rolling and lifting hot water crust. This procedure is also easy with practice. The first few times are a bit fraught. When it is in place, firmly pinch all around the top. You can do this before or after you trim the excess pastry, it is a matter of choice. In any case when you have finished pinching a very neat border go around again pushing the edges up vertically with a knife. This makes the finished pie look crisp in appearance and prevents burning of the thin edges.

6. Roll out the trimmings thinly. This is when the artist in you is let loose. A well decorated pie top sells the product. A dramatic but simple-to-do design requires a wavy pastry-cutter. If you run it over the pastry using a ruler as a guide you can achieve dozens of strips of about a quarter of an inch in diameter. Lay these strips diagonally across the pie at two-inch intervals; do the same in the opposite direction. Instant Tudor lattice-work appears. Whatever design you choose, you must have space for two air-holes. An apple-corer is ideal for making these. You want them to reach right down to the bottom layer of sausage-meat. You can decorate the edges of the holes or leave them plain. The great moment has come and the pies are ready for the oven.

7. Pre-heat the oven to 190°C/410°F/Gas 6. Put in the pies. Cook for half an hour, then paint beaten egg thickly over. You can put the egg-wash on before it goes into the oven if you do not wish to touch the hot pie; we always find we get a better glaze if we wait until the pastry has set. Turn the temperature down to 180°C/350°F/Gas 4. The pies will require at least another hour and three-quarters. If you peer into the holes in the pies you should see clear juices, if they are still coloured leave the pies a little longer.

8. Take the pie out and leave it to stand for half an hour. This is where food poisoning accidents can happen. The aim is to pour aspic into the pie so that when it sets the jelly nicely holds it all together and makes it even more delicious. Problems occur if the jelly, which is very susceptible to contamination, has become contaminated. This is what you should do. Having made a savoury jelly, a pint or slightly more for each pie, make sure that it sets by putting it into the fridge. When you melt it, either melt it over hardly any heat at all until it just melts or heat it thoroughly and bring it back to the boil. Do not warm it to hand-hot and then use it. Pour it slowly through a funnel into the pie. It will pour down, finding the spaces. Fill until you can just see it through the holes. Then put the whole pie to cool as quickly as you can.

9. To turn the pie out, loosen all the edges with a knife. Put a thick folded dish-cloth on the surface and turn the pie out on to it. The decorations on the top will be fragile so this requires some care. Although the whole procedure seems lengthy, it is actually

very simple to produce ten or more pies in a batch when you are practised. Fan-assisted ovens greatly decrease the required baking time and are worth considering if you intend to produce a lot.

Poacher's Roll

This is a simple recipe for turning good sausage-meat into a roll that can be cut for pubs or buffet-catering. As well as making it with pork, we produce one using a venison sausage which is called Gamekeeper's Roll.

Method

1. Make one pound of shortcrust pastry. Use a recipe with less fat than usual (about 3 oz fat to 8 oz flour is ideal). Roll it out into a long oblong about a quarter of an inch deep.

2. Put one pound of sausage-meat, mixed with an egg and a tablespoon of flour, in a line down the centre. Now close up the parcel. You can do this by folding the sides over and clipping the ends or tucking the ends in like making a bed. Either way, trim off any excess pastry so that there are no doorsteps at either end. Seal the joins with water.

3. Turn the whole roll on to a greased baking-sheet and brush over with egg-wash. Put two slashes on the top to let the steam escape. Bake at 185°C/400°F/Gas 6.

With practice these rolls can be made very quickly. We make our pastry in a food-processor in batches and then assemble it in batches. Even a normal domestic oven will bake a dozen or more of these rolls in one go. If you decorate the top with cut-outs, the rolls are very attractive on a cold table. They can be served cold or reheated. The pastry reheats very well in a microwave. The smell of these rolls reheating is delicious.

Variation: For a different flavour, mix an ounce each of chopped onion and chopped mushroom into the sausage-meat.

Making Bacon

To make acceptable bacon is one of those country occupations that provides a multitude of options. At one end of the scale it is a long, complicated ritual resulting in beautifully smoked bacon happily lasting for months in an airy place. At the other end it is an instant process producing bacon for family consumption after only a night's preparation. This latter bacon will only 'keep' in a deep freeze. Traditionally, bacon is made from a heavy pig, but we often turn joints from a lighter, pork-weight pig into bacon. The smaller pieces are easy to handle and they cure more quickly than large pieces.

A Sweet Cure

(For 15 lb pork — back legs make ham, front legs make fore ham, belly makes streaky bacon and loin makes back bacon.)

For the pickle:

1 lb black treacle	1 pt malt vinegar
½ lb block salt	2 pts old ale
½ lb brown sugar	1 tablespoon saltpetre

Mix all the above ingredients together until well dissolved.

1 lb coarse salt for rubbing the pork.

Method

1. Take the pork and rub it well all over with the coarse salt, rub it particularly thoroughly into any areas from which bones have been removed. Rubbing the salt into the meat tends to 'cure' bare hands as well, so it is worth wearing rubber gloves.

2. Put the meat into a brine crock — to be really ethnic a stoneware crock is ideal — failing this, a plastic bucket will do the job just as well. A piece of wood cut to fit the container will prevent the meat from rising up out of the brine.

3. Pour the cold pickle over the pork. Turn the joints twice daily for the first week and then once a day for four weeks.

4. Drain the meat for 24 hours. This is most effective if you hang the joint up in an airy place. Dust the dry meat with rice flour, put it in a cloth bag and hang in a cool airy place. Cured like this the hams are at their best in six months, smaller pieces like belly can be consumed immediately. In any case, this is a mild-flavoured

cure and the meat should not require soaking before cooking.

Smoking

To take bacon making to its ultimate you must resort to smoking. Cool smoking uses the chemical nature of the smoke to solidify the albumen in the meat and turn it into a very stable product. Smoking is often a dramatic affair. We have many exciting memories including setting fire to a great wooden hogshead when we attempted smoking in too high a wind. When we eventually managed to rescue the sausages we had been attempting to smoke they were definitely barbeque flavoured! The most satisfactory way of slowly smoking large hams is to construct a smoke box high up in an inglenook chimney. The temperature for cold smoking must never go above 90°F or the fat will start to melt. High in an open chimney the hams can slowly acquire a golden glow. Without the inglenook you must make a smokehouse. This can be any sort and size, an upturned barrel over smouldering wood shavings is a simple beginning or if you have an old defunct outside lavatory these can make excellent permanent smokehouses. If you live near a commercial smokery you may be able to get your cured products smoked. We once had some mutton hams smoked by continental sausage smokers. The resulting hams were spicy and delicious. In fact anyone who was not told the origin of the deep red meat thought that it was an excellent silverside of beef, which was pretty good as the mutton had come from two aged rams. Commercial smokers are available to buy in this country. They look rather like large fridges and have automatic smoke and temperature settings. They are often advertised in *The Field*. The great benefit about these regulated smokers is that you do not have to keep leaping up in the middle of the night to check that the fire has not gone out! Hot smoking is very popular in the USA. It is simply cooking in hot smoke. It does not preserve the food, but simply gives it added flavour.

Instant Bacon

In the early evening thinly slice a pound of belly of pork. Lay it in a dish and sprinkle it with two ounces of sea salt and trickle a tablespoonful of honey over it. Just cover with water. Turn the slices over a couple of times during the evening before going to bed. In the morning drain the meat, rinse under a running cold tap and then dry. Fry or grill and serve with some lightly fried free range eggs — delicious!

RABBIT

Here is a favourite recipe for using rabbit — with a French flavour.

Rabbit pâté

1½ rabbit joints	black pepper and salt
1 lb belly pork	grated rind ¼ lemon
3 slices streaky bacon	4 juniper berries
1 small glass brandy	2 bay leaves
2 cloves garlic	2 oz butter or pork fat
good pinch dried thyme	
good pinch ground mace	2 pt pâté dish

Method

1. Cook the rabbit in a covered casserole just covered with water at 350°F until just tender. Assuming this is a home-produced young rabbit it will be ready in half an hour or so. If it is an aged breeding doe or a bought rabbit of doubtful vintage it may take an hour. When cool enough to handle strip the meat from the bones and cut it into thin strips. Rabbit bones splinter easily so keep a watch out for chips of bone — these do not add to the pleasures of eating pâté.

2. Coarsley mince the pork and mix with the rabbit, crushed garlic, thyme, mace, pepper and salt, lemon rind, crushed juniper berries and brandy. Cut the bacon into strips, put half in the bottom of the pâté dish, pile in the mixture, level the top and cover with the remaining bacon and the bay leaves. Cover the dish — tin foil makes a good airtight seal. Put into a bain marie and cook at 300°F for one and a half hours.

3. Take out of the oven, loosen the tinfoil so that it touches the surface of the pâté and put a weight of about 1½ lb on top. If you have used a round pâté dish a side plate with a large can of baked

beans on top is ideal. Leave overnight to set. The next day cover the surface of the pâté with melted butter or pork fat. This pâté keeps for a few days in the fridge.

JAMS

When faced with a large quantity of fruit to preserve for the winter our grandmothers, without the choice of putting it all in the deep-freeze, turned to producing jams and bottled fruit. Today we eat jam because we like it. We do not generally hoard vast quantities of it to last us through the cold months. Most jam sells in the summer and most of it appears to be eaten in the summer as well.

The aim when producing jam for sale is to produce a fresher taste than that available from the supermarket shelf. A look at the contents of most of the jams available today shows that in many cases jam-making is a chemical process in contrast to the romantic image of jam-making in years gone by. If the fruit you have available for jam-making is of good quality and you are prepared to spend time and energy in producing a good product, the jam will be delicious. How does the public find that out? Sometimes the public will buy jam because of where it is sold. We sell some of our produce through local stately homes that are open to the public. Visitors are looking for something to buy and jam which is clearly locally made sells well. The jam stands out as being locally made because we say so on the label. For anyone to appreciate that your produce is special it must say so on the label or on a suitable display. A totally handwritten label can prove this but the lettering must be large and legible; the jars must also be uniform.

It is not suitable to collect old jars all year and then fill them, using cellophane lids. To start with, the local standards officers will probably dislike this presentation. Apart from that, if the cellophane lids get punctured, which can easily happen, the jam will become contaminated. The easiest jars to obtain commercially are honey jars. Because honey clubs are spread all over Britain, these jars, half pound and one pound size, are widely available. Until recently, it was possible to obtain powder jars — the jars that chemists use for creams. They have a range of lids to fit and if a pretty cloth lid is put on, they look attractive. However, it seems that these jars are now only going to be available on special order. It may be worth asking your local chemist if he would like to buy some with you, then you should get a bulk discount. The price of jars can vary widely and since they are a very costly item in jam production, it is always worth asking several local suppliers for quotes.

The label itself is another area where you can spend a lot. A small quantity of printed labels is always expensive: you have to pay for the plate cost and if the design was done for you, the origination costs. The more you order the more the original costs are diluted. However, you may not wish to commit yourself to several thousand labels for Strawberry Jam. There are several alternatives to consider. The first is to have one master-label, without any variety on the label, no contents and no weight. If you do not put any weight then as long as you select a suitable size for the label, you can use it on large and small jars. This label, which is really just a label with a decorated border carrying your trading name and address, has to be filled in before use. There are two ways to do this. It is sometimes worth having the labels over-printed if you are producing a large run of one product. A printer can do this or it may be worth considering buying a small print machine to do it yourself. The other way is to write the labels by hand. They must be clearly written and the size of the lettering must conform to current EEC requirements. We have produced hundreds of handwritten labels over the years. Although it sounds unbelievably tedious, it seems to get fitted in around other jobs. It is possible to have all your labels produced by photocopying. Many of the print shops in towns have excellent copying machines that produce very clear images. If you have the copying done on to coloured paper, a very personalised style can be achieved. The master-sheet can be done totally by hand or you can construct the lettering and often an attractive design using some of the instant lettering available. You simply position the lettering and rub it off its plastic backing on to the paper. The initial artwork does not have to be the size of the finished article. In most design studios the artwork is initially far larger than the required size. Using a reducing machine (you may have to visit several print shops to find one), the artwork can be reduced down in size or even up.

This produces a very professional finish to hand-drawn artwork. Even if you feel you are not an artist it is worth trying several layouts to see if you can produce a label you like. Unless you are prepared to leave the design totally in the hands of a designer you will want to be very involved anyway. The product should look appealing; it should also portray the image you want. It is possible to buy ready-printed labels as you would for jam to store at home. These labels must be large if you intend to use them for retail sale and again you will need to write them by hand. Try the pen and ink you intend to use on a piece of label first and see how it reacts to damp. Many outlets suffer from condensation and if the ink runs you will get all the jars handed back when you call for a repeat order.

Certain varieties of jam always sell well. The standards like strawberry and raspberry will sell and in some locations special lines, like damson with almonds, will sell as well. It is more dangerous to overproduce than to underproduce in cash terms. Once the jam is made you have to sell it to obtain your return. It is often worth freezing a stock of fruit that you can process as you get the orders. If you do this for the first year, you can judge your market without the danger of having several hundred jars of jam stored without sales.

There are two main types of jam recipes to use at home. The first is the traditional fruit and sugar collection of recipes. The second are the recipes based on using added pectin. The case in favour of the first is that the longer cooked jam has a traditional, slightly caramel flavour and, if you grow the fruit, you are only concerned with buying the sugar and the occasional lemon required in some recipes. In the pectin recipes the flavour of the jam is lighter. This flavour is often preferred by younger buyers who may well never have tasted traditionally made preserves. Obviously you must buy the required commercial pectin and with these recipes timing the boilings is essential. With the first method it is temperature that you must keep checking.

In any sort of jam recipe you will require a lot of sugar. This is one of those commodities that it is impossible to buy cheaply. Buying from a supermarket brings a few pence off per kilo. Going to the extent of ordering a great bulk of sugar from manufacturers gets you very little reduction in price. Whether you buy your sugar in bulk bags or simply in one-kilo bags therefore makes very little difference to the price and the decision is based on whether you prefer dealing with a bulk commodity or opening lots of little bags. The main argument in favour of little bags is that if you do happen to spill a bag you are not spreading some twenty-five kilogrammes about!

Traditional Strawberry Jam

To make one batch in a traditional large preserving pan, you will need the following ingredients:

Ingredients
7 lb strawberries
juice of 2 lemons
6 lb sugar

Method
1. Take all the greenery from the berries and wipe them well. Some strawberries have mud splashes: these make the jam cloudy and gritty. If you have to wash the berries, wipe them dry.

2. Put the berries and lemon juice in the pan and heat slowly so that the berries start to give out juice. They will need some simmering to become soft. If the fruit is very ripe this will not take long.

3. Add the sugar and stir gently until it is dissolved. Do not let the pan come back to the boil until all the granules are dissolved. Then boil rapidly to 220°F. It is always worth checking that the jam has set when this point is reached. Put a little jam on to the back of a saucer and stand it near the window. It should wrinkle when you push your nail through it. Turn off the heat and remove the pan. Take the scum from the top, using as flat a spoon as possible. If the fruit throws up a lot of scum while boiling, drop in a tiny knob of butter. This makes skimming easier.

4. Let the jam stand for about ten minutes: this helps to keep the fruit distributed throughout the jam. Now pot the jam in sterilised jars and put on the lids. Always fill the jars right to the top of the jar.

Strawberry Jam using Commercial Pectin

Ingredients

4½ lb strawberries   6 lb sugar
juice of 2 lemons   1 bottle pectin

(Check that your brand of pectin specifies similar quantities to the above.)

Method

1. Clean the fruit and squash well using a potato-masher. Put in a preserving pan.

2. Add the lemon juice and sugar. Heat gently, stirring until the sugar is dissolved. Add a small knob of margarine, bring to a full boil and boil for three minutes. It is important that the pan is boiling all over its surface. Often a big preserving pan will boil madly in one corner while another is just simmering. You may need to adjust the position of your pan on the heat source to achieve a full boil.

3. Take the pan from the heat, stir in the pectin and skim. Allow to stand for ten minutes then pot.

These two recipes show the kind of difference in the types of recipes. The pectin-assisted set is much quicker to produce. As well as making jam using commercial pectin, you can make the pectin yourself from a high-pectin fruit such as apples. To prepare pectin stock from apples, you will need:

Ingredients
10 lb chopped whole apples — with cores
3½ pts water

Method

1. Simmer the apples in the water until tender. Strain off the juice and put it into containers.

2. Next day, add another pint and a half of water to the apple pulp. Simmer for an hour, strain and mix the two juices. You can use the pectin stock immediately or sterilise it in bottles to keep.

Strawberry Jam using Home-made Pectin

Ingredients

6 lb strawberries
6 lb sugar
¾ pt pectin

Method

1. Put the strawberries and the sugar in a preserving pan. Heat gently to dissolve the sugar.

2. Add the pectin stock and boil until a set is reached. Pot as usual.

JELLIES

Jellies sell best if the recipe you use produces a suitable flavour for eating with cold meats and pies. Although fruit jellies can be eaten as an alternative to jams, this market is far smaller than that of selling to delicatessens and specialist food shops. This means generally that the jellies are sold in half-pound pots or even smaller pots and that the labelling should give suggestions about how the jelly should be eaten. Apple jellies flavoured with herbs, such as sage or thyme, are very suitable in this market. Redcurrant jelly is a standard line and cranberry jelly sells well at Christmas. If you have access to rowan berries, you can produce a traditional jelly for serving with game. Very often small batches of unusual recipes sell — for example, bitter orange with cloves and lemon with thyme.

Traditional methods of making jellies involve preparing the fruit, cooking and straining, and boiling the juice to a set with sugar. Time of cooking is reduced using pectin. The initial cooking and straining can be simplified using a steamer. If you do use a steamer you must be careful not to over-dilute the fruit. A few sample runs with the equipment you have will show the kind of juices you want to aim for. You can do this on a trial and error basis, that is by making the jelly and seeing if it sets well. Or you can use methylated spirit to test the juice for pectin content. Take one teaspoonful of the juice and add three teaspoonfuls of methylated spirits. Shake it well, leave for a minute and then gently tip it into a cup. If it is all in one large jellyish mass, you have a juice with a high pectin content; if there are several large clots, the jelly will still set. But if there are lots of little clots, there is not enough pectin. If the fruit was steamed to produce the juice, the steamer was probably left on for too long. If you followed a specific recipe and strained the juice then the fruit you are using is probably low in pectin.

Traditional Apple Jelly

Ingredients
12 lb cooking apples
2 lemons
sugar as necessary

Method
1. Chop up the cooking apples; you do not have to remove anything, they just need to be clean. Put them into the pan with the juice of the lemons and with enough water to nearly cover them and gently cook until they are tender. Some cooking apples obligingly break down into a nice soft pulp. Other varieties may require some encouragement with a wooden spoon. When the pan contains a nice soft mess empty it into a strainer. How you strain will probably be governed by the amount you are processing. It is very ethnic to tie a square of muslin to the legs of a chair, upend the chair and balance a container in its centre. Then you put the pulp into the muslin and leave it all to drain overnight. We did that very many years ago in the warm kitchen of a farmhouse in Devon. When we came down in the morning we realised that we had forgotten to evict the cat for the night. The result was one furious cat who had spent the whole night licking apple pulp from herself and no juice in the bowl but lots on the floor. If you have similar hazards either use a steamer, in which case you do not have to separately strain the juice, or at the least make muslin bags that hang from hooks and do it somewhere nobody wants to go for hours.

2. Measure the juice that you have made. For every pint of juice, add one pound of sugar. Stir to dissolve and boil to setting point at 220°F. Skim and pot as usual.

Apple Jelly using Commercial Pectin

Ingredients

6 lb cooking apples	6½ lb sugar
3 pts water	1 bottle pectin

Method

1. Make the apples and water into juice as in the above recipe.

2. Take 4 pts of juice and put it in a preserving pan with the sugar. Stir to dissolve, adding a little knob of butter. Add the pectin and bring to a boil for one minute. Again as the cooking time is so short it is important that the whole pan is boiling enthusiastically.

3. Remove the pan from the heat and pot.

Both of these apple jellies can be flavoured by adding dried herbs or whole spices. Do not add ground spice or dusty herbs because these will make the jelly cloudy.

CONFECTIONERY

One of the most traditional flavours of the country is captured in home-made sweets. On traditional British summer holidays, where you often dress more for the wind than the sun, a piece of home-made fudge turns many a wet day into a happy one. Our sweets — the fudge and coconut ice — are all warmers. Take possibly Britain's most internationally appreciated confection, that delicious mint ice from the Lake District: it is clear that our skills lie in providing a supply of sugar for the system. Home-made fudge in general is crystalline; for all the careful boiling, the various recipes and methods evolved, it is unusual to get a creamy one. The first recipe here is the answer. Follow it exactly and the result will be a soft, creamy fudge that cuts and keeps well. The next recipe is for the more usual type. Both fudges sell very well in the summer if you package them in cellophane bags with little labels. Some customers want a boxed fudge but they are very much in the minority. We have also successfully sold it in slabs for cutting in the shop. You can vary the flavours using different additives. The usual varieties include rum and raisin, coffee and vanilla. How about muesli? That is very simple: just add some spoonfuls of your favourite muesli mix. To be really different, you can pour a layer of melted chocolate on top of the fudge. But if you call it chocolate fudge make sure that it is. If you buy cooking chocolate it may well be another substance, referred to as 'compound' in the trade. If you use this you must call your product 'chocolate-flavoured'.

All fudge cuts best if you score it when it is warm and then use a very thin knife with a firm stroke to cut it. Professional fudge-makers use a circular knife that they roll to cut with. This gives an even pressure. Your fudge may have a high moisture content — look at the bottom of the fudge after it has been sitting for a while' are there damp marks? If there are, it has a high moisture content. The cure for this is to age the fudge a little in a dry atmosphere — overnight in an airy room usually does the trick. If you bag damp fudge, it will go gooey.

Creamy Fudge

3 lb granulated sugar
1 lb 2 oz golden syrup (this is easier to measure when warm)
13 oz condensed skimmed milk (this is one large can. Do not use full cream milk.)
13 fl. oz water
15 oz butter
3 drops vanilla flavouring
5 oz fondant, cut into little pieces (this is obtainable in little bags as fondant icing or in bulk from a baker's suppliers)

Method

1. Put the sugar, golden syrup, milk and water into a heavy-based pan; the pan must be large enough to accommodate three times this volume. Very gently dissolve the sugar, making sure that every grain of sugar is dissolved before bringing to the boil. Boil to a temperature of 235°F.

2. Add the butter and the vanilla flavouring. Stir to mix the butter in and then boil to 245°F.

3. Take off the heat. Allow the mixture to cool to 200°F, then add the fondant. Stir to dissolve the fondant and keep on stirring

until the mixture starts to thicken and go paler in colour.

4. Pour the mixture into a prepared mould and score. Leave to set.

Note: It is important to keep a continual eye on temperature. The usual danger area is in the cooling before the fondant is added. It seems to take for ever with the fudge loitering somewhere around 220°F. So of course you look less often, only to find that the pan had dropped to 170°F. All is not really lost but it does take a lot more effort to get the fondant to dissolve.

Traditional Fudge

Ingredients
2 lb sugar
1 pt milk
2 oz cocoa
¼ tsp cream of tartar
few drops of vanilla essence
4 oz butter

Method
1. Slowly dissolve the sugar in the milk in a pan. Add the cocoa and cream of tartar. Boil until the mixture reaches 238°F.

2. Take off the heat, quickly stir in a few drops of vanilla, drop the butter on top of the mixture and leave the pan alone until you can start to see that the mixture is beginning to set around the edge. Now stir hard and enthusiastically until it starts to feel heavy. If you are producing this in a big batch go on until you feel as though you cannot do any more. Put at once into prepared pans, score and leave until cold.

Leaving the butter not stirred in until the last minute does give you the creamiest result of all the more traditional recipes. If you are going to add any fruit or nuts, add them at the last minute. If you want to use home-produced milk, this recipe is very suitable. You can use a very hard clotted cream in place of the butter but it does have to be hard — a normal double cream will not give you a good result.

Coconut Ice

You can use home-produced milk to produce coconut ice.

Ingredients
4 lb sugar
1 pt milk
1 lb 8 oz desiccated coconut
flavouring
colouring (optional)

Method
1. Dissolve the sugar in the milk in a pan. Boil hard for ten minutes.

2. Take off the heat, stir in the coconut and flavourings. (You can use flaked nuts in place of some of the coconut as a variation.) Choose your own flavourings. If you use grated orange or lemon peel the product is more sophisticated. Flavouring with real brandy and grated orange and mixing chopped ginger into the basic recipe is also delicious.

3. Add the colouring if used. If you want the traditional two-colour coconut ice, pour out half the mixture, colour the remainder and pour that on top.

4. Leave the ice in a cool place to set, marking deep lines where you want it to cut before it is quite hard. A warm sharp knife will cut most effectively — using a sawing motion helps reduce the amount of crumbs made on cutting. If you are wrapping before sale, cellophane makes the product look its most attractive.

CHEESE

Cheese is traditionally made in a dairy. It is quite possible, of course, to make it in the kitchen although for storage and to mature you will need a stable, cool temperature. In the winter the cheese may need some heat or it will drain too slowly.

If you have never made cheese before, it is simple to build up some confidence by making some quick cheeses for home consumption. The very simplest way is to drain soured milk. On a warm summer's day milk will sour quickly all by itself; on a cool day you can help it along by adding lemon juice or vinegar until it starts to curdle. Now tip the whole mass into some muslin and put it to drain. In a warm room this will only take an hour or two. If it is cold, it may take all night. If you are in a hurry, you can squeeze the bag but then some of the cheese will force itself out into the whey and the cheese you have made will be rather tasteless. Add some salt, then some chopped herbs or lemon juice. Or beat in some castor sugar and eat it with fruit. Although this curd tends to be tougher than the more slowly made cream cheeses it can taste delicious and when mixed with eggs, fruit and sugar will make delicious old-fashioned cheesecakes. It is too tough to make fine American cheesecakes, the uncooked variety of cheesecake that is widely available today. Anyway, there is a lot that can be done with it and it is cheese, made at home.

A blander tasting product can be made by draining yoghurt through muslin. In Germany this is called 'quark' and you may find an elaborately packaged fruit version of this in the supermarket. The flavour of the cheese depends on the milk used to make the yoghurt. If you use a goat's milk yoghurt, the cheese has an acid tang. Very often people buying British goat's cheese are disappointed at the mild flavour compared to the powerful stuff coming from other countries. One reason for this is that often our goat's cheeses are sold very fresh. The other may be that the continentals keep more billys than we do. The presence of billy goats is said to make the milk taste far stronger. (This does not imply that the milk is contaminated.) Certainly goat's milk that we have bought in France had a far stronger taste than ours and this was the only factor that was really different in our management.

To make cheese with rennet is the next logical stage. If you are producing the milk from your own animals, make sure that it is as free from contamination as possible. If you are buying the milk, buy from a reliable source. If the milk has been pasteurised, you will have to use a 'starter'. This can be bought from health shops if you are aiming to produce on a small scale or from a dairy supplier if you require quantities. Starter is added at the rate of half a drachm to one gallon of milk. Two gallons of milk will make four cheeses of about one pound each in weight. One drachm of rennet is required for one and a half gallons of milk. To add the rennet it should be well mixed with six times its volume in water and then mixed very thoroughly into the milk. The milk should be at about 92°F when the rennet is added. The best cheese is made from the evening's milking and that milk is in a suitable state to use the following morning. When the rennet is well stirred in, start to stir only the top of the milk until you can see that the milk is coagulating. Cheese rennet is much stronger than the rennet used in making junket which is why such apparently small quantities can set such a large volume.

Everything that cheese is made in must be absolutely clean or the cheese will pick up unpleasant organisms. You can buy specialist cheese hoops to mould in or use other objects from the kitchen. A deep flan ring, one with no lip, will make an ideal mould. Straw mats are traditionally used to drain the cheese on but paper-cloths will work. Once the milk is set, you ladle the curd into the moulds — simple, short-keeping cheeses do not require the curd to be cut. Using a saucer, ladle the curd into the hoops, filling to overflowing. As the cheese drains it will sink. Leave the cheese to drain. The temperature in the draining-room should not rise above 70°F or fall below 65°F.

After twelve hours turn the cheese over very carefully on to a clean straw mat or other material. Keep turning the cheese at twelve-hour intervals for several days. Possibly after 48 hours it will be solid enough for you to remove the mould. As a matter of taste, you can salt each side of the cheese as you turn or not. This cheese is ready to sell or eat as soon as it is firm. The problems associated with this kind of cheese production are all related to the unfortunate fact that it is a very perishable product. If you can sell the cheese from your own premises or are selling to retailers who appreciate the specific handling required, you have less problems. To try to sell this cheese into a shop where there is no specialist knowledge is probably to invite problems. Ideally the cheese should not be covered in any way; if a mould forms on the surface it should be wiped off. The cheese should be turned regularly. Ideally you should return to the age-old tradition of producing such cheeses for sale wrapped in a fresh cabbage leaf. The leaf provides drainage with its shaped ridges, coolness and protection from flies and dust; failing that modern packaging is a compromise.

A semi-hard cheese can be made by carrying out the same initial stages to achieve coagulation but then cutting and heating the curd. Specialist knives are available for cutting the curd or you can use a carving-knife and a little dexterity. The aim is to cut horizontally and vertically, producing squares about one inch across. When the curd has been cut, leave it for a few hours to start to drain. The squares of curd will now be slightly shrunken and floating in the watery looking whey. The aim now is to raise the temperature of the whey to 100°F. If you are making a small quantity of cheese and your container is heat-proof then it can be gently warmed on a cooker to the required temperature. If your container is not suitable for this or the quantities involved make handling difficult, take out jugfuls of whey, heat that above 100°F — but not above hand hot — then return it to the remaining curds and whey. Continue until all the whey is up to 100°F. Leave to cool slightly. Now drain the cheese, put the curds into a rough cloth and leave them to drain. Whether you further break the curds or not depends on the texture you are aiming for. A moist cheese requires large pieces of curd and vice versa. The next day add salt to taste and put the cheese into its mould. A deep cake-tin is ideal. The mould should be lined with cloth and then you should weight it. Putting four cans of baked beans on to the pressing board is ideal. Keep turning the cheese as necessary. If it looks as if the cheese is progressing well then leave the weights as they are. It may be necessary to add more if it looks as if the cheese is not compacting well. When the cheese is firm you can remove it, unwrap it and prepare its final appearance. Give the surface a good wipe with a rough cloth then bandage the whole tightly with fine cloth. Mix a flour and water paste and seal all the edges. A very thin layer of melted fat applied to the bandage gives a nice finish. Put the cheese to mature in a temperature of 55-60°F.

You can use this basic recipe to make many different flavours of cheese. The flavour depends on the milk used, whether the aim was to produce a moist or dry cheese and the amount of salt added during manufacture. If you make a fairly moist cheese, you may find that it blues during storage. The most delicious cheese we have ever made was a natural blue made with Ayrshire milk. Although it is hard to get an absolutely regular flavour using these recipes, they do produce very attractive cheeses for sale.

YOGHURT

There are several different brands of small yoghurt-makers on the market; they all help to keep the milk at a suitable temperature for yoghurt-making. You can make large-scale insulated boxes using polystyrene insulation to maintain a fixed temperature for yoghurt-making.

The method of making yoghurt is simple. The aim is to slightly evaporate the milk used and then to curdle the milk using a specific culture. Boil the milk, preferably in a double boiler, for half an hour. This evaporates it a little. It should not be at a rolling boil but just at boiling point. Cool the milk as quickly as possible to 113°F. Mix it with the culture. Put it into the insulated container and leave for six to twelve hours.

The culture can be specially obtained from a dairy supplier or you can start with a carton of commercial natural yoghurt. In any case the culture does not remain true to type for long and should be renewed if any 'off' flavours form.

Bees

Keeping bees is one livestock enterprise that can be practised almost anywhere. The delicious honey produced by suburban bees still manages to evoke images of flower-laden orchards and country lanes. There are even beehives in the City of London — though not very many. The bees survive on window-boxes and the small oases planted as picnic-places. The great thing about bees is that they fly off to gather food for the hive and so they do not have to be right in the middle of a food supply, just within reasonable striking distance. Apparently, one bee makes about 2,000 trips to flowers to make one teaspoonful of honey: that is something to remember as you spread it thickly on the bread at tea-time.

In commercial terms, bees produce honey and beeswax and, of course, more bees. To sell good honey is not difficult: the price is always good and there are very few areas where enough is produced to meet local demand. Anyone who appreciates using beeswax as a furniture polish is a good customer and anyone who does not appreciate it has probably never tried it. If you want to sell the bees you produce as a beekeeper, you either need someone who is going into beekeeping from scratch or another beekeeper who wishes to expand his enterprise more quickly than his own bees will allow. You may well be your own best customer for the first few years but eventually you will end up with some surplus bees unless you just let them swarm and fly away which is wasteful and in populated areas unpleasant and possibly dangerous. There are not very many people who are allergic to bee stings, something like one in a thousand, but nobody likes being stung. You should bear this in mind when you come to site your hive near your neighbours properties. Bees will fly up high over an obstacle so if the hives are in a suburban setting or in a populated country setting, put a high fence a few feet from the hive. This means that the bees will rise into the air and tend to disperse rather than treat neighbouring gardens as a fly-path.

Bees may not find enough food in a newly developed area. Although established suburban gardens are usually good feeding-grounds, large areas of newly cultivated gardens are not. Water is another attraction for bees. We had friends whose suburban goldfish pond became a buzzing cloud of bees on summer evenings. Granted they had a delightfully flowery garden with herbs and shrubs as well but it appeared to be the pond that was the great attraction. It became quite unpleasant at times and clearly young children could no longer be allowed to play about in the garden. The problem was never solved as the neighbours with the hive had no children and not much sympathy; eventually our friends moved house so we have no idea of the final outcome if there was one.

Whether you intend to start bee-farming with one hive or to buy an existing bee-farm on a franchise basis (the newest method of honey production), it is important to find out whether you can get on with the bees. Traditionally bees do not take to fornicators! Nor do they like sweat or dirty clothes. Putting together all that, pure, sweet honey is clearly best produced by pure, sweet people! It is up to you to judge whether you fall into this category or to decide to take a chance if you do not.

Many beekeepers are happy to show you some of the intricacies of beekeeping. If you contact your local bee-club, you will be put in touch with someone suitable. Getting stung is never pleasant, even when you have developed some degree of immunity as you seem to with several stings. If the thought of being stung fills you with horror, do not go in for bees. Even honey is not worth it. However, if like many people you are fascinated by the intricate workings of the hive and you are prepared to put up with the occasional sting, you will probably find beekeeping one of the most fascinating occupations.

HIVES

Left to their own devices, bees will as happily build a nest in a hollow tree as in a purpose-made hive. The purpose of a man-made hive is after all simply to make it easier for you to remove the honey and to ensure that the honey is as free from impurities as possible. When a honey-eating bear raids a hive in the wild he is not concerned about pieces of bark and the occasional insect, neither does he have to ensure that the honey is clean enough not to ferment in storage. We all assume when we take honey from a jar that it is pure and wholesome and the best start to producing clean honey is to have the bees in a suitable hive. Manufactured hives are quite similar in design and if you intend to make your own hive, it should have the same basic design.

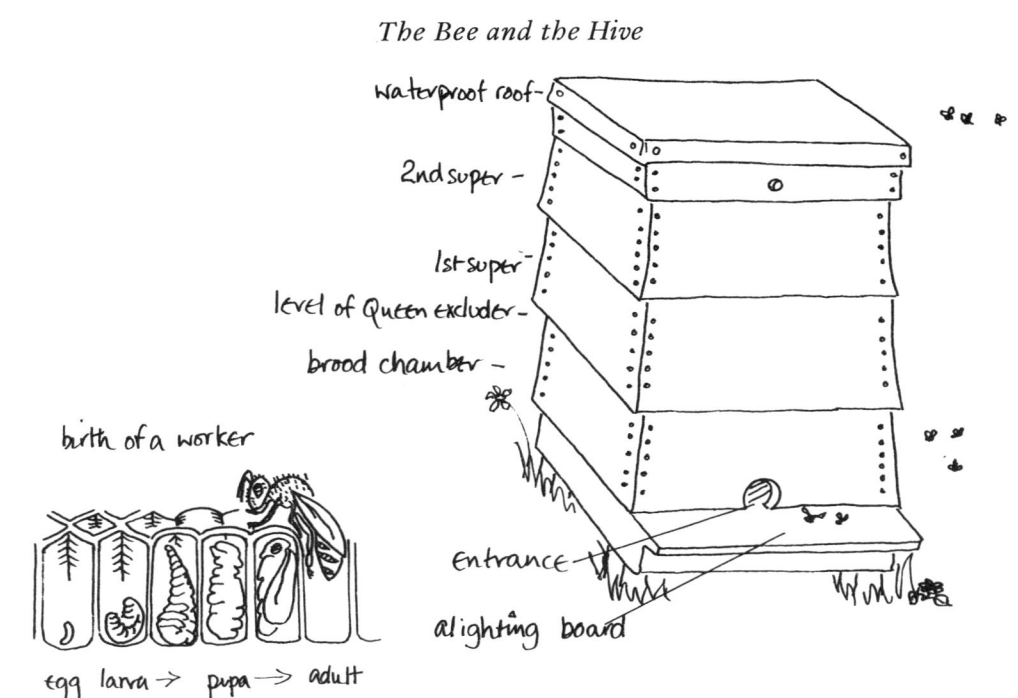

The Bee and the Hive

- waterproof roof
- 2nd super
- 1st super
- level of Queen excluder
- brood chamber
- entrance
- alighting board

birth of a worker

egg   larva →   pupa →   adult

Starting from the bottom, where the bees enter through a small hole, the first layer is the brood chamber. This is a rectangular box, open above and below. On the bottom it rests on a board and above it, there is a screen with holes that are small enough to allow access for the worker-bees but too small to allow the queen to pass through and lay her eggs in the honey storage boxes. The queen is thus confined to the lower box which is referred to as the brood chamber. In this she lays her eggs and here the worker-bees feed the larvae.

When the workers store the honey in the second layer they are providing us with our crop. Left totally to their own devices, they are simply building a reserve of food to last them through the winter. When we interfere and take some honey, we have to supplement their diet as necessary with sugar.

Hives generally have two storage layers, referred to as 'supers'. When these are both full, a third layer can be added. On top of this high-rise bee-house is a roof to keep out the rain. The hive should have ventilation holes at the top. In the winter you should put a mouse-guard at the entrance hole; a bee-house is just as desirable a residence as a human house to an autumn mouse, no doubt even more so as it is crammed with delectable honey. The mouse would not last long as the bees kill intruders but the carcass is too large for them to remove and is therefore a possible source of infection. What the bees would do to counteract this is typical of bee ingenuity. They would form a layer of propolis over the dead intruder. This is the substance collected from leaf buds by the industrious bees. Being resinous, it is a strong glue and is used in hive construction; it is also a natural antibiotic and would help to prevent the decomposing mouse from infecting the hive.

Really competent woodworkers may find constructing a hive part of the overall challenge of keeping bees. The rest of us are probably best advised to buy one. You can often buy second-hand hives and it is also possible to construct fairly simple outer boxes and simply buy the frames to hang inside them. Some enterprising beekeepers convert dustbins to use as hives. These are apparently very successful, even if they look somewhat unromantic. The most romantic hives of all are the original straw skeps that our ancestors used. We in fact use a drawing of one of these on the honey fudge that we sell. They are certainly less productive and we use the modern hive in reality to produce the honey. In any case, whatever kind of hive you decide to use, you can be sure that for each hive occupied this year you can expect to fill another with bees next year when your bees swarm.

OTHER EQUIPMENT

Having got a hive, empty and ready for use, there are a few other items you will need. One of the appeals about beekeeping is that the necessary equipment is fairly limited. One item that you will most certainly require is a smoker. This is simply a pair of bellows attached to a funnel; you fill it up with something smokey such as old rags and have it poised for action when you handle the bees. If the bees become agitated, the cool smoke calms them without damaging them. What a shame that no-one has developed something similar for dealing with irate humans. You may just wish you had such a device if your bees swarm in a neighbour's garden!

Another item you will need is a hive tool. This is made of steel and has a flat blade at one end and a scraper at the other. You can often find something similar in your tool box. If you do, make sure that it is quite clean before using it. You use it when you want to open up the layers of the hive and when you want to get wax from the frames.

As you are keeping bees to remove some of their honey, you must replenish their larder in the winter. To this end you require a feeder of some sort. There are several designs available. They all contain sugar syrup that you make up. If you want to sell or eat honey and wax together, you put lots of little boxes, referred to as sections, into the supers instead of the usual larger frames. The bees are never quite as enthusiastic about filling the little boxes, presumably because being sociable little creatures they prefer working in large groups. However, in a good year, you will get quite a reasonable yield this way. You will also receive a premium for honey sold in this way and will avoid having to purchase the second most expensive item of equipment in beekeeping after the hive — an extractor.

You need the extractor to extract honey cleanly and efficiently. An extractor works on the same principle as a spin-dryer, using centrifugal force to remove the honey from the comb. The honey must be clean before you jar it or you will find that it ferments.

Very nice if you are making mead but not if you are selling pure honey. Some groups of beekeepers share extractors and sometimes you can hire one through a beekeepers' association. Clean honey jars are a necessity and if you are producing a lot of honey, you will need to buy some new jars. In any case, you should always use a new lid to avoid contamination. You can ask your local beekeepers' association about obtaining jars.

That is about all you need specifically apart from clothing. The delightful prints of beekeepers working with flowing veils is not simply rural romance. Protective clothing is a necessity. A wide-brimmed hat with a veil that falls on to the shoulders should always be worn when handling bees. Wear close-fitting cuffs and always tuck your trousers into your socks. Long, flowing skirts on female beekeepers look extremely ethnic but the action of several furious bees trapped inside the folds requires very little graphic description. Even very experienced beekeepers seem to become lulled into a false sense of security and we have heard the most unpleasant tales of some such souls who simply omitted to tuck in their trousers. Not only do a multitude of stings make you feel painful and sometimes quite ill, there is also the sad knowledge to be gained that the hitherto friendly little bees are really no respecter of persons. Whether you wear heavy gauntlets or not is really a question of choice. Bees do not like being roughly handled and will show it; on the other hand, to handle bees with bare hands requires a degree of confidence that many of us do not possess. Remembering the fact that bees dislike dirty clothes and sweat, whatever protective clothing is worn should be cleaned periodically. It is also inadvisable to wear strong-smelling perfume or aftershave. In a modern world it is surprising how many strong-smelling substances we smother ourselves in. Deodorants, hair sprays and fabric conditioners are often overlooked as being strong-smelling aggravations to the sensitive bee.

OBTAINING THE BEES

You can get started into beekeeping in three different ways. The first, and most dramatic, is to capture a swarm. This usually comes about when you have been put in touch with a beekeeper who is aware that his bees are about to swarm and who no longer wishes to enlarge his numbers. The early summer is the most usual time for this awe-inspiring migration of bees. It is all part of the complex nature of the hive. The queen suddenly departs with up to half the adult population of the hive. A watchful beekeeper will have been keeping an eye on the emergence of young queen larvae within the hive. These are identified by the size of cell and the position they occupy within the hive: the cells are bigger than those of worker-bees and instead of lying horizontally they hang vertically. If you have been put in touch with a suitable supplier at this stage, you must be totally prepared to act quickly when called. Your hive should be ready for occupation and the supers should contain wax-filled frames. You also require a feeder as the newly moved bees should be cosseted on their arrival to enable them to establish themselves.

When the call comes you dash off, complete with protective clothing, to capture the swarm. If you cannot bear the excitement of doing it yourself, you should pay the seller an extra fee. It is worth remembering, however, that from now on you are going to be dealing with those bees yourself, so you might as well be in at the beginning. A swarm of bees is an intimidating sight. When they are in flight they emit a booming sound. Fortunately they swarm on to something, often a branch, fairly close to the hive before taking off altogether. This is when you want to effect your capture. Sometimes, of course, you are not swift enough; then the bees are off and wherever they swarm to next — they are there for the bold to take them. Years ago a swarm appeared on our village green. The entire village rushed around like bees disturbed, some wanting to find the beekeeper responsible, some trying to find someone brave enough to capture the swarm. By the time suitable brave souls had materialised the swarm had departed. Nobody saw where they went but the village was supplied with excitement for the day.

When bees are in a swarm they act as a mass and are not very difficult to capture. You advance with a box, place it under the swarm and sharply bang their resting-place. Hopefully the whole swarm will drop into your box which you can hastily cover and make away with, at speed, to your own hive. Once there, you make the opening to the hive as large as possible and place a ramp of wood leading up to it. You then turn the box upside down at the bottom of the ramp and tap it to remove any lingerers. The bees with luck run up the slope and enter the hive. Usually they are quickly installed; you then close the entry to a gap of about three to four inches wide, attach the syrup-filled feeder and retreat, feeling unbelievably bold. Now you can celebrate. When you discover that the number of bees in the hive is decreasing, do not despair. It is simply that it takes a while for the newcomers to multiply and replace the bees that are naturally dying of old age. After a week or two, remove the feeder and in a few weeks you can watch the hive multiply.

The second way to establish yourself with bees is certainly less dramatic as you are not involved with a capture. On the other hand, you are faced with the sudden responsibility of owning and being responsible for some 40,000 bees. When you buy a colony of bees from a dealer you should obtain a queen, ten combs, a brood chamber, some honey and pollen. In other words, you are soon going to be in business. Whether you are going to obtain honey this year depends on the time you buy your colony. Obviously, if you buy early in the year, you may get honey that year. If you buy late in the year, you will not.

The third and final way to start is to buy a nucleus. This consists of the same range of bees but on a smaller scale (slightly less than half). This is a slower way to get going. If you are a little tentative about beekeeping then this is going in at the shallow end.

LIFE IN THE HIVE

It is difficult to decide where to start when describing the inter-related organisation of bees in the hive. Philosophers and lesser mortals find the essentially complicated relationships in the community a source of morals and some confusion. If we start with the queen we are at least starting with an individual. She is indeed treated like a queen: she is fed and groomed. Her sole occupation is to provide eggs for the hive; she has no hand in the rearing of the young. Usually a queen will lay about 1,500 eggs a day at the height of summer. It is possible for her to lay up to 3,000. She herself grew from an egg laid by her mother. The egg was laid in a particularly large cell and was fed on a diet of royal jelly. If she had not had this special diet, she would simply have developed into a worker. She would not have been the sole virgin queen in the hive. However, she would have been the first to hatch. She then had to kill her competitors. After this somewhat violent arrival she rested for some five to ten days. The old queen left the hive, complete with around half of her followers, as the young queen came to maturity.

This brings us to the next bee participant in the collective life — the drone. A drone is a male bee; he leads a delightfully sheltered existence, being fed by the workers, until the day comes for him to fulfil his destiny. This is to fly out from the hive, meet and fertilise a queen. Often this occurs between bees from different hives. Drones that do not mate return to the hive and venture out another day. Successful drones do not return. Mating kills them. As the summer ends returning drones are prevented from entering the hive. The workers no longer feed them and they die.

Workers are unbelievably industrious bees. The worker is a female born into a life of hard service. Initially she is a house-bee; she grooms and feeds the queen and cleans the hive. Later she moves on to the business of collecting pollen and nectar from flowers. A solitary bee would need to gather 37,000 loads of nectar to make 1 lb of honey: this proves how essential it is to keep your bees happily multiplying. The worker processes the honey and makes the essential combs from wax produced by special glands. She is a most conscientious worker and even regulates the temperature of the hive by enthusiastic wing-fanning. All this effort is crammed into a life of some six weeks — presumably the workers die of exhaustion! The larvae that exist in the brood chamber are fed on a kind of bee-milk. This is produced by the nurse-bees who process pollen that has been packed into comb cells by the worker-bees. It is nectar that is converted into the honey we eat. As the bee returns from gathering, enzymes are already at work converting the nectar to easily digestible sugars. The bee regurgitates this mixture into a cell of the honeycomb and it is sealed over with wax. In its own little hexagonal cell the honey matures. The airflow from the wing-fanning worker-bees evaporates some of the water contained in the cell. This is essential to the keeping of honey. If you gather the honey too soon while its water content is too high, you will find that it will not keep without fermenting.

PRODUCE FROM THE HIVE

Producing honey is one of nature's delights. You kill nothing to produce one of the finest foods available to man. The work must necessarily be carried out in an unhurried manner or the bees and therefore your production levels will suffer. Even when you have supervised all the work carried out on the hive yourself and handled your bees for years, you are still presented with a feeling of mystery when dealing with honey. There are innumerable legends and items of folklore about honey and bees. Honey is said to help a number of illnesses, including arthritis and bronchitis. Apparently, the Phoenicians called Britain the Isle of Honey.

For all its centuries of use and appreciation, honey has still not been conclusively analysed. There is still a small percentage of the contents that has not been classified. There have been attempts to produce honey from the known constituents but this has not been successful. Clearly we require bees to make our honey as much as we require them to pollinate our crops. If you live in a fruit-growing area, you may be able to find a farmer who will actually pay you to put your hives in his orchards to pollinate his fruit. This is indeed a bonus; your bees get free access to nectar-rich fruit blossoms and on top of that you are paid for their efforts.

To sell good, clean honey is often just a question of putting a sign at your gate. In many areas, especially if you are keeping bees in an urban environment, this is sufficient to sell surprisingly large quantities. In country situations you may have to take your produce to shops or other outlets. Make sure that the label clearly shows that it is pure honey and where it was made. Customers like to know where the honey came from and a pretty label will help your jar to sell if it is in competition with others. Honey as it comes from the hive is in liquid form; you can either sell it like this or sell it when it crystallises, as all honey will eventually. The honey can also be sold in honeycombs produced in sections (see p. 176), or you can put slabs of cut honeycomb into a jar with some extra clear honey. Beeswax can be sold as it is to a knowledgeable market or you can process it into furniture polish or candles.

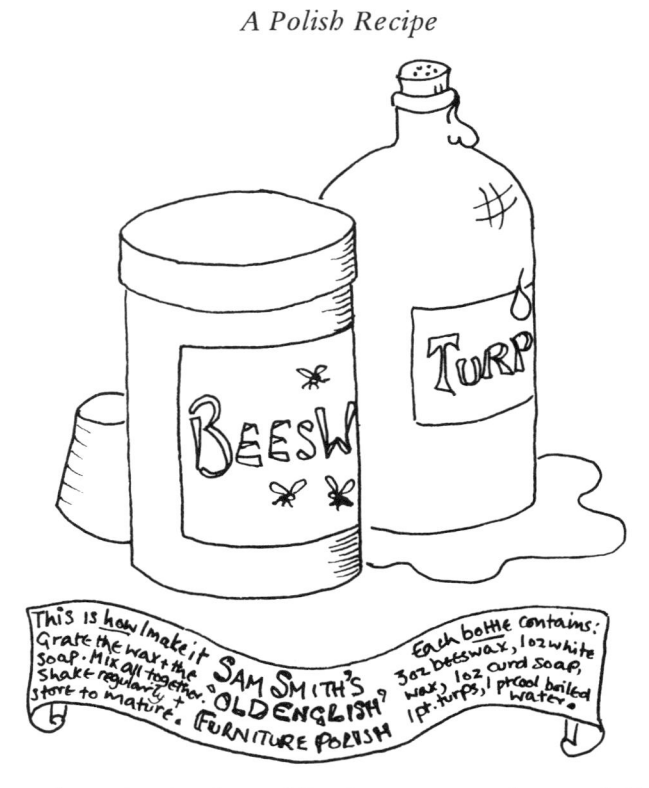

A Polish Recipe

This is how I make it. Grate the wax + the soap. Mix all together. Shake regularly. Store to mature.

SAM SMITH'S OLD ENGLISH FURNITURE POLISH

Each bottle contains: 3oz beeswax, 1oz white wax, 1oz curd soap, 1pt. turps, 1pt cool boiled water.

One way of proving to the public that your product is different — put the recipe on the label!

There are two other items that come in smaller quantities from your hives. One is propolis which is the resinous substance used for cementing within the hive. This is a natural antibiotic and some hive-owners concoct mixtures which apparently have healing powers. Finally we come to royal jelly, the food that turned a potential worker-bee into a queen, so powerful that during the five days that the queen was in her larval stage her weight multiplied 1,500 times. This substance has always been the source of unbelievable claims for rejuvenation and beauty treatments. Although the claims seem incredible, there may, of course, be an element of truth in them. If this is the case, perhaps the best use that can be made of the tiny amounts of royal jelly available is for the beekeeper to consume it himself.

Honey Products

The sweetness and flavour of honey makes it a saleable product. Anything made from honey — cakes, fudge, mead — always retains an essentially wholesome flavour. Beware when sampling your mead; all mead-makers have tales of its potency and most of them are quite true.

Wax Products

Beeswax can be sold to manufacturers of polish and candles or you can make your own polish and candles for sale. The illustration opposite gives instructions on how to make polish.

Wool

Pure wool is warm. Straight from the sheep, it contains naturally waterproof lanolin and probably twigs, dirt and bugs. Having obtained a whole fleece, it has to be spread out, preferably on to a clean sheet, to have all the bigger alien bits removed. When the fleece is laid out before you it is easy to recognise the different bits. The tops of the legs and the thick neck wool clearly show the shape of the animal. In a short-fleeced animal there may not be much difference in the length of the wool; in a long-wooled sheep it will be short where the legs are and longer in the body. Some fleeces feel soft to handle and are lustrous to look at. In others the kemp — the rough hairy bits — are all through the fleece.

The suitability of the fleece for processing is governed by several factors. If you are intending to spin the fleece, the governing factor is your own ability. Some people take to spinning like ducks to the water. Others never quite get the co-ordination of foot and hand going. To be able to produce spun yarn is very satisfying. Taking a fleece and transforming it into clothing is one of the most basic fulfilments. There are other ways to use wool. You can simply pluck out tufts of wool from a long-haired fleece and knit them as you go. The result can be spectacular using a coloured fleece. You can pull out long fibres and use them to embroider plain cloth. Or you could put the whole fleece between two pieces of cloth. Sew squares on the cloth to anchor the wool and you have an original padded coat. Stuffed toys using wool are soft and washable as are cushions. If you are allergic to feathers or rather to the mites that live in old feathers, you may find that stuffing cushions with wool is more acceptable.

Before you spin you generally use items called carders to make the wool into uniform rolls called rollags. The action using the carders, which carry lots of bent pins in opposite directions, is to roll up light fluffy coils. These coils can then be spun or you can knit directly with them or apply them to other fabric with a couching stitch. Although usually wool is only seen as a product after it has been spun, there are many other possibilities for using it in a raw state. If you can manage to spin a little wool, why not stretch that on a frame and weave tufts of wool in and out of it? If you pack this wool in tightly and turn in loose ends you will quickly make beautiful thick hard-wearing rugs. If you can use multicoloured fleeces like the Jacob's you can stagger the shading and produce a work of art. A small amount of wool can be spun as the Egyptians did using a drop spindle. Or you can be even more rustic and use a potato as the weight. Spinning-wheels themselves are attractive pieces of furniture. They have variations in design and are often local in origin. Once spinning by hand was an essential part of our survival. Today it is a craft. Many hand-knitters would pay well for hand-spun wool. You can often learn to spin at local evening classes. If there is not such a class near you perhaps it would be worth advertising for a teacher. The most surprising people can spin and often are delighted to show newcomers how to begin. Although an experienced spinner will judge their ability by the fineness and evenness of the yarn they spin, it is often most appealing to the knitter when spun in an irregular manner. The differing thicknesses make most attractive jumpers. Truthfully if you want really even wool, it is produced by machine; even the Jacob wool is spun commercially if you want this kind of continual evenness. To weave is another country enterprise that can be wool-based or today use man-made fibres or linen thread.

The basic principles of weaving are easy to acquire. With a full textbook and a simple loom it is no time at all before you are able to construct simple pieces. The most awkward parts initially are chaining the warp and then fitting it to the loom. This process really needs two pairs of hands. If help is available, all that is lost is your temper. If not, you will have to employ the aid of odd things such as chair-backs; at least there is nobody to see the first hair-raising attempts. The width of fabric you can produce is entirely governed by the width of your loom. It is always advisable to buy the widest loom you think you will need from the outset. Otherwise your work will be limited.

A Table Loom — the width of material is limited by the width of the loom

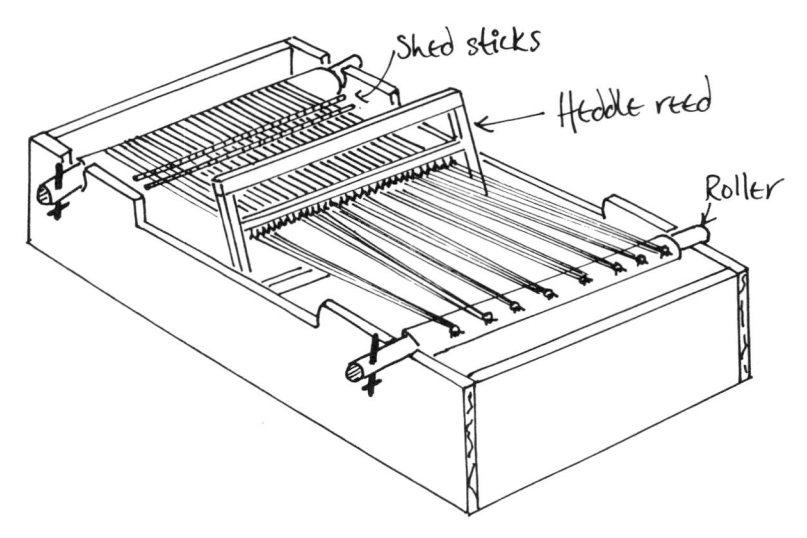

[Diagram of a table loom with labels: Shed sticks, Heddle reed, Roller]

There are two main outlets for woven work. One is to dressmakers who require hand-loomed cloth for special pieces. The other is to sell specifically woven pieces as works of art. All sorts of varied colours and textures can be worked in. Several prominent artists in this field specialise in wall hangings that evoke country landscapes and sunsets. Advertising in craft magazines may bring commissions and certainly word of mouth advertising will help. It is becoming quite usual for companies to use hand-produced tapestries in board-room settings. If your work is not suitable for a wall hanging, perhaps it is suitable for a special set of curtains. Craft outlets often require you to leave your work on display with them. They then pay you if it sells and deduct a commission. This kind of exposure may get you a reputation in an area but it may not be sufficient to provide an income. Often customers such as the board-room commissions will not approach you but will respond favourably to an approach. It is worth constructing some moveable samples. It may be difficult to describe adequately the speciality twelve-foot-long hangings you have in mind: it is easier

Simple Spindle Spinning

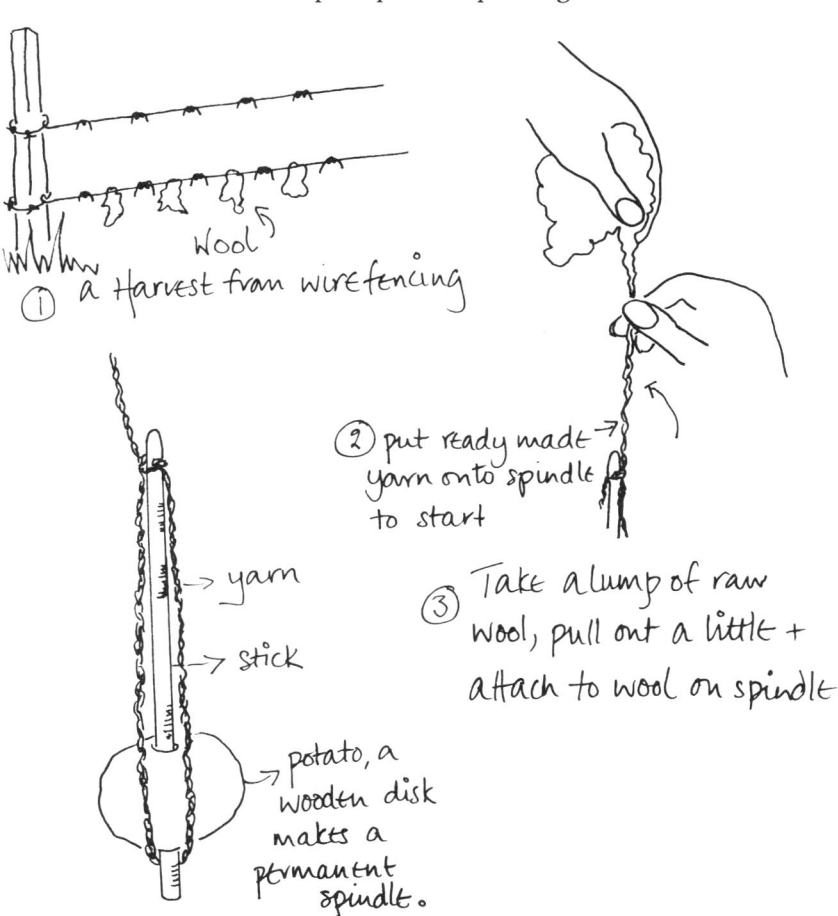

① a Harvest from wire fencing — Wool

② put ready made yarn onto spindle to start

→ yarn
→ stick
→ potato, a wooden disk makes a permanent spindle.

③ Take a lump of raw wool, pull out a little + attach to wool on spindle

④ Set spindle spinning clockwise

⑤ Tease out wool between thumbs, let go with bottom thumb, twist runs up. Repeat until spindle reaches the floor.

⑥ Now you're spinning as the ancient Egyptians did! Wind spun wool around stick of spindle + start again.

with a one-foot-square sample in front of you.

There are sometimes local exhibitions in town halls and other centres at which you can show your work. These can all help to establish a reputation. Some craft shows are very good at attracting custom but some are very poor and it is always worth checking on planned advertising and the past experience of the organisers before paying a fee for a stall. Better still is to negotiate a percentage fee for your stall. If you feel you cannot justify a position on your own, it is often worth sharing space with another craft worker. It is all a question of exposure to get the reputation and asking for orders to get the business.

Water

Depending on the amount of water on your property and where it is situated, water can be viewed as an asset or a hindrance. Water is an asset if it falls, nicely and regularly, on your growing crops: that depends on where you live. Water is an asset if it is contained in well defined natural storage areas such as ponds and streams. If the streams are strong enough to power an electricity-producing device then that is certainly an asset. If you have several large expanses of water, these can be classed as assets if you intend to farm fish or to rent out duck-shooting. If the water is contained in a heavy waterlogged soil, it is a hindrance.

The way to drain land depends firstly on the location and slope. If your land is on a good slope, it may simply be a case of clearing out old ditches or digging new ones. Dropping ditches by an extra foot in length can sometimes have a dramatic effect on the land; so can providing a proper exit for the ditches. Many ditches do not lead into sufficiently deep removal areas so that water stays in the ditches instead of being led away. The only reason to have permanent water in a ditch is if you intend to irrigate the land from it. If you are trying to drain the land, make sure that the ditch empties. You may have to consider mechanical draining. There are various grants available on some land for this and it is worth seeing if your land is suitable. Another cause of waterlogged land is running stock on it. A field that has naturally poor drainage turns into a mud-bath when stocked with cattle or, in particular, shod horses. Horses are almost always bad for the land. They do not graze efficiently and tend to poach favourite areas. Even sheep have to be kept off wet land in the winter. Over the long term it is worth building up the humus level of your soil and letting earthworms help you to aerate it. All the cures for waterlogged soils are time-consuming. In desperation you could always cover it with concrete. There is one area in the West Country where many small farms have unbelievably large areas of concrete. It was put there by successions of farmers who moved there because the land was cheap. They soon found out why: it was wet and the local farmers had the land values correctly fixed.

A Water Wheel

'Free' power

Moving water can be channelled into a small width to provide a race that can then be harnessed to provide electricity. In its most romantic form, this is achieved by a water-wheel, rurally churning away. This could provide you with enough electricity for most of your needs; you can supplement its use by boosting your water-heating with solar power. In a less romantic sense, any conglomeration of movable pieces can turn things. Many Heath-Robinson devices produce power from water. If someone got down to refining one of these devices, there might be a good sale for them in suitable areas. Moving water can also be used to fill fish-ponds to farm fish. The essentials for farming high oxygen consumers such as trout are fast-moving water and plenty of food. With slower fish like carp the water can be relatively static. A good bubbling spring may well provide the kind of water required for fish-farming. Possibly more exciting still, you may be able to bottle it and sell it as spring water. However, this requires all sorts of licences and permission. That is not surprising: after all, what you think of as a spring may be something fed from your neighbour's septic tank — that is a bit of an exaggeration probably but not impossible! There has just been a case of a health inspector quite happily doing his job and following the supplier of some bottled water bought in a supermarket back to its source. Although the product was beautifully bottled and labelled, he discovered to everyone's horror that the owner of the spring had been merrily putting it into bottles without applying for any licences and without knowing its source.

Close to centres of high population, one of the most valuable pieces of water you can own is a fishable pond. Coarse fishermen are the largest group of sportsmen in Britain. They sit out, sometimes all night, in pouring rain around stretches of water that would otherwise yield no income whatsoever to the owner. This kind of activity has to be monitored or all the locals will happily fish for nothing while your visiting, paying fishermen complain about overcrowding. Often one of the easiest ways to get over this is to let your fishing to a group. Many companies have angling clubs. Although you may get a marginally smaller income, this means that they instead of you have to worry about the water being fished by non-paying participants.

Shooting wildfowl is often best approached on the same basis. Here the people you are allowing on your land are dangerous. If they do not hit what they are aiming at they may hit something else and it is worth checking out references or at least making sure that they can hit the proverbial barn door. You may be advised to watch this from some distance through binoculars! If you do allow access to your land then your responsibilities to keep various dangerous places such as mine-pits well guarded are increased. A written sign is not enough: children and others might not read. Even if the mine-shaft does not belong to you, and many are in separate ownership from the land, it is still up to you to make the area reasonably safe.

Flighting Ponds

A sprinkling of small ponds in pasture makes ideal duck flighting ponds.

Enormous stretches of water can suit many different occupations: fishing, water-skiing and so on. The problem is generally to keep conflicting interests apart and to make easy access to the water. Again it is easiest to run the organisations as groups but the trouble then is that you may be excluding from use of the water the very people who would put it to best use. There are several firms of advisors to consult about use of your land — some of the large estate agents have specialists in this leisure field.

If your problem is that you do not have enough water, your aim has to be to conserve every single drop that falls on your property. For a start, even water-butts at the bottom of drainpipes can collect considerable quantities. Large areas of roof are excellent catchment areas. Rain-butts can be put at the end of every building, shed or greenhouse. We have several old galvanised water-carriers that push along on wheels. Although our problem is often too much water, we find them invaluable in the summer. Really large water storage systems need to be well protected from wandering children — that is to protect the children. Also from passing geese and other pollutants — that is to protect the water. Although the ecology in a natural pond copes happily with the droppings of a few water-birds, an unpopulated water-tank does not. Very quickly the most unpleasant bugs start to develop in its depths.

Marketing and Selling

PRESENTATION OF THE PRODUCT

Having decided on the product you are going to produce, you now need to spend a few hours thinking about how you are going to make the enterprise more likely to succeed. Put your produce somewhere where you can really look at it. Now stare and keep on staring: look round it, at it and under it. There are several points to be considered. The first is: who will use it? If you are going to receive money for whatever you are producing, cheese or wool or anything, someone other than you is going to use it. Now who will pay you to use it? We can all give away excess French beans, but who is going to pay you for your specifically grown ones? Are you aiming to sell direct to the user or someone in the middle? The someone in the middle can be as obvious as a retailer or possibly someone who intends to alter the product before it is then sold again. For example, you may find a customer for spun wool who intends to weave it into cloth before selling it. Who among the prospective purchasers you can think of will pay you the most money for the product? Will the same customer give you repeat orders or would the product have to be cheaper to encourage continuous business? Perhaps you can only ever produce enough to satisfy one-off, expensive purchases. Or perhaps your enterprise depends on selling regular amounts to long-term customers who buy on price. The latter category clearly applies to the egg trade. For regular custom to be worth reducing your price for, it must be reliable. It is difficult to raise your price successfully more than simply to keep up with inflation. Some produce, such as pork, rarely manages even those price rises. To have a successful pork enterprise often means having to weather troughs in the market. This is one of the reasons why we process some of pork into pies: this way we can lift the income from our product.

Having fixed your ideal customer in mind, the object you are looking at now requires packaging. Everything requires some packaging, from a 25 kg sack of potatoes to a few ounces of pot pourri. With joints of pork or even a half-pig, the packaging is simply a label. But something must go with your product, if possible to enhance it and certainly to keep reminding the customer about where it came from. With some products there are legal requirements; the EEC lays down sizes and type of labelling for many products. Generally these are obvious, such as having the contents clearly visible, and the size of printing has to be sufficient to show up clearly. Sometimes the rules have their own reasoning. For example, if you went to school some years ago you may be tempted to put the required metric weight using the abbreviation grms. Do not! You will immediately be pulled up by your local weights and measures department; you must put g or the whole word, nothing else.[1] When you take a product such as jam it is clear that it must be sold in a jar. At first the appeal of a pretty-shaped jar, seen on retailers' shelves, may seem to make the choice easy. It does not. For a start, to obtain an unusually shaped jar you will probably be asked to order hundreds of thousands. This is because big manufacturers do. It is rare to be able to purchase small quantities of unusual jars. The only way we ever manage it is when we are offered the ends of 'runs', or more often imported jars. It seems odd but it is easier to find fancy foreign jars in small numbers than British ones. Most surprisingly, they are cheaper too. If you come to the decision that you will buy standard jars then clearly you must make the labelling stand out from your competitors. This is where you have to come to another major decision. You are in this enterprise to make money. Is the packaging that you feel necessary for your product going to increase the value of the product sufficiently to cover packaging costs? Will the packaging you envisage sell more of your product? That is after all your aim, that your attractive packaging will help to sell your product and give you a good return on the investment of your time and money. It is always possible to give suitable products a seasonal boost by using special packaging. At Christmas we produce

196 / MARKETING AND SELLING

Examples of Some Effective Labels

a special mustard mixture, put it in larger jars than usual and put on a festive label and a shiny paper lid tied with gold string. This product sells well by itself but it also helps sales by selling the small jars as well. Having brought mustard to the customer's attention, they can then choose to buy the festive special or a cheaper jar from our usual range.

Distribution puts strains on your packaging. If you are intending to sell and deliver yourself, the product simply has to arrive in good condition in a manner suitable for the customer. For example, if you are delivering pre-cut and wrapped pork straight to the housewife for her freezer, you can deliver in a plastic tray that you take back with you. If your product has to be delivered by carrier or if the final recipient is a big chain that will further shift your goods, the packaging must be robust. Cardboard boxes are astonishingly expensive. If you have to order ones with a specific measurement, these are the most expensive. It is worth enquiring as to the sizes a manufacturer carries in stock and even going round several manufacturers to see if you can obtain suitable cartons without having to go to the expense of having them specially made. Sometimes you may be offered boxes that have already been overprinted for another customer. There is a paint that will cover this kind of printing and it is often worth the extra labour for the saving in packaging costs. The stage before considering carton printing yourself is to apply printed sheets to the carton. This can look extremely effective and saves committing yourself to the cartons being printed. After all you may wish to package something different in your cartons one day, then you have to overpaint your own printed cartons!

So the final product has appeared at last. The produce had been turned into a product by choosing its market and applying the necessary packaging. This packaging may well change with time and as the product finds its level in the market. Sometimes a good product needs additional help to boost sales. An organisation that made very good yoghurt was just ticking over. The usual price competition took up most of the selling time. They decided to go for a stronger brand image and bought the rights to a children's TV programme image. The difference in sales was spectacular. Now they were not simply selling a yoghurt, they were selling an image. Although this is a large-scale story, the same type of success can come when you hit the ideal image for your product. It is after all the image that the customer buys, whether that image is yours because you are selling it direct, or the product image as it sits on a shop shelf. Finally, what about your own image as you back up the product? The only rule that seems to cover successful direct selling and talking about your product is to be nice. That might sound soft, it might sound stupid in a business sense. But it is true. When you are producing a home-produced article, your buyers want to feel that they are buying something different and that they are having a pleasurable experience. From the retailer you may call on to the buyer who comes to you, be nice to them. Sometimes this is the most difficult part of the whole enterprise! It does not mean being soft if someone complains unnecessarily, it just means being pleasant and interested that someone is bothering to buy your produce. After all, without customers there is no enterprise.

SELLING OPERATIONS

To make a successful sales and marketing plan, you have to reassemble the list of assets which you compiled at the beginning of this book. The assets remain the same but the emphasis will be different. It is time to honestly assess your ability to make the product you intend to sell and to decide how big a quantity you can really produce. With something simple like pork, the figures speak for themselves. You know how many young stock you have and, with reasonable allowances for casualties and slow growers, you can come up with a fairly accurate projection. What you will not know until you have had several batches of pigs slaughtered is the type of grades you can achieve. To obtain the best price in any market you must produce lean pork of the correct weight. If the first results are disappointing, it is clearly worth trying to improve your regime because the only increase in income you can produce from a fixed number of livestock is the bonus you receive for producing the very finest end-product. If your enterprise has more fluid end-results, for example turning soft fruit into jam, your production is fixed very much by your own ability to produce. When you have produced large batches of jam over a period, your production rate certainly increases: this is partly due to increased ability and partly due to increased confidence. Initially the thought that some 24 lb of jam may not set tempts you to go on boiling for far longer than is necessary. Sometimes, in fact, this overboiling spoils the end-product. Again, practice improves production levels.

A major factor in deciding how much marketable product to produce is the capital you have available. With the livestock enterprise the initial capital requirement is clear: you must buy the young animals and spend any money necessary to make their living quarters satisfactory. Also, you must have money available to cope with the feed costs you will incur before the animals provide you with a cash return. There also has to be an allowance available to cover unexpected costs such as vet's bills. All these are limiting factors to the size of the enterprise and therefore the quantity you are aiming to produce. Also, of course, the time you have available has to be considered. If you aim to spend all day looking after your pigs, you could aim to keep hundreds; if you are aiming to feed, water and clean before and after work, the enterprise is necessarily limited. Applying the same kind of conditions to a manufacturing enterprise such as making jam gives you similar limits but the limiting factors are more the other way round. Because the amount you can produce is very much tied to the hours you have available to stand cooking, time is the most limiting factor. If you grow the soft fruit yourself, you only have to fund the jars and packaging. If you intend to produce from bought fruit, it is worth remembering that you can almost always buy ready-picked soft fruit more cheaply than 'pick your own'. It is one of those odd facts that if you buy either through a wholesaler or from a street market, you can usually get the best price. Of course, you have to ask the street trader for a bulk price and you may have to wait for the end of the week to get the best price when he has stock he does not want to keep over a weekend. If you buy regularly from a wholesaler you will probably get better terms than if you buy spasmodically. You may be able to pay on a monthly account when buying from a wholesaler which will help your cash flow.

Having decided how much of your intended product you will be offering for sale, you must now examine the market-place as it exists at this moment, taking into account any factors that may change it by the time your product will be ready. The first factor to consider is the geography of the area in which you live. Selling is easiest if you have a large suitable market on your doorstep; unfortunately, this is not often the case. In very many instances, craft workshops that have been set up in converted agricultural buildings all over the country have found this to be one of their biggest headaches. Clearly talented people are producing excellent products but ventures fail because the products are not sold. It is therefore imperative to decide from the very outset exactly where and how you will sell your produce. If you spread a map out on the floor, mark your own location and then the location of places you think are suitable sales areas, a clear picture will start to emerge. There may be special circumstances that you should take into account. If, for example, you make a regular trip, say some twenty odd miles away each week, does this take you through a suitable selling or delivery area? Do you live on or near a busy road that could bring business right to your door? It is relatively easy to come up with a lot of relevant assistance in your normal life when you are relaxedly contemplating a future enterprise. The whole process becomes far more difficult and steamed up when you have a garage full of product and an irate bank manager.

The actual method of delivery of the product is one that must be considered. Clearly if you aim to deliver fresh meat around the country, you must have specific transport. If your product is jam then the main limiting factor is weight. A small car will carry more volume than you think but it will not cope with the weight of a few hundred jars of jam. The sales of your product are further limited by its presentation and the selling ability of whoever actually asks for the order. Look honestly at the product as you intend to sell it. For a start, would you buy it yourself? Compare it with competitive products: does it stand the comparison? Unpleasant though this may all sound, it is much better to do all this privately, well away from your intended customers. You can avoid a lot of unnecessary criticism if you really make sure that the product is as attractively presented as you can make it. Apart from anything else, whoever sells the product will have far more confidence in it if it appears to be professionally produced.

The selling ability put behind your product will certainly affect sales. That does not mean that it need be presented by a super pressure salesman. No-one expects or wants that when the product is intended to be country-based in its appeal. There are several sales methods that will help to achieve your aim of exchanging your product for a customer's money. When you have decided who is to sell your product, look at pages 107-8 and decide how many ways you want sales to be assisted. This may well affect the amount of money you need to be available before your product brings you a return.

A further thought is that in a small country-type business, whether it is craft or production of foodstuffs, you often get a far better response from your customer or prospective customer if he knows that he is dealing with 'the boss' or at least someone involved in the business. For a start, the customer can expect to receive clear and specific product knowledge, even if that is as simple as what type of chickens laid the egg! It is also pleasant for the customer's ego: it shows that the person selling the product is eager to actually talk to the customer. As a person involved in the whole production and sales of the product, you can 'get alongside' the customer. There is more to this than a simple sale: the customer should feel more involved and therefore more satisfied with a purchase and more prepared to buy again.

The simplest way to bring the seller in contact with customers is to have a farm shop; this does not mean that you have to live on a farm or that the product has to appear as if it came from one. It is simply a question of having a base at your place of production where the customers can come to you. The customers can either be the general public or you could establish a cash-and-carry service for retailers if your product is suitable. Taking this type of project further, you could take on premises in a local town or village as a base or possibly share premises with another producer. When we took a farm shop in a local village, we spent hours trying to foresee what people would buy most of and working out how we could keep up production. When the shop was open, we felt compromised by the continual requests for things which we did not stock and actually went out and bought them. In the long run it was the home-produced things that sold and many of the bought-in commodities that we used ourselves. You have to be very strict with yourself and follow the plan you worked out initially or the essentials of the enterprise get lost in a kind of general shopkeeping. Direct selling from your own premises works well (especially if the produce is food) if you are able to remain open at times when other shops are closed. If the demand for produce is quite light, it can probably be coped with alongside production. If you find that your site is one of those sought-after commodities — a gold-mine — you will either have to consider opening the shop for limited hours to allow yourself to carry on more production or you will have to staff the enterprise with extra help. Then, of course, you will have to work out if the wages you pay that staff are definitely covered by the extra business. Hopefully they will be and you will be getting an extra profit as well. If you are producing craft items, it is easy to find that you get a lot of admiring people filling your work time and not too many buyers. Then it is definitely worth having fixed opening times and keeping a very close eye on the sales you make. It may prove most economical to sell away from your production area and not to allow the public access.

If you have dismissed the idea of having a farm shop or have decided that you would at least have to supplement sales, you must approach the market-place. When you produce meat you can do this in several ways. Local agricultural markets will sell live animals for a low commission; usually the payment is within two or three days. It is well worth asking around to find out which markets within reach of your enterprise achieve the best results in your field. We do not use the most local market to us for selling cattle. The difference in price achieved by going a little further outweighs the extra transport costs. Many agricultural markets hold sales of dead poultry and eggs but always check on the kind of returns you can expect before sending in your produce; once it is sold you may regret the low return. There is often a technique in using these local markets. Very often one year's last-minute low turkey prices at Christmas means that the opposite will happen next year. Everyone hears of the bargains that were to be had last year, they rush along in Christmassy mood to snap up a bargain and eventually the prices go through the roof. We have just had a year like that locally. Next year everyone will stay away and it will be the time to buy.

A surprisingly large number of butchers will buy meat direct from you (not the chains, of course: they buy centrally). What you have to check is that the price offered by the butcher covers what the slaughter-house would buy from you at plus the slaughtering charges. With poultry, of course, these conditions do not apply. Your meat production may or may not need to be regular throughout the year to satisfy these customers. Some butchers will happily buy 'one-offs'; others will only buy if you undertake to supply on a regular basis. When you are producing fruit and vegetables, your customers will accept that there are seasonal variations. Some greengrocers like their carrots supplied with no greenery; others become highly agitated if the fern is not attached. All these little points need clarification. If you intend to sell eggs, it is absolutely essential to be regular in your supplies and to fulfil the sizes required. This will almost always require some buying in of supplies through the year but if you do not do it, another supplier will and your business will be gone. Milk and cream and other dairy products have seasonal fluctuations in demand but there must always be sufficient to meet demand. You can take milk totally out of the 'rat race' of competitive selling and sell exclusively to the Milk Marketing Board. If your premises are suitable for direct sales but the area around you is not, it is often worth advertising for custom.

Craft-type produce requires a different market. Craft shops themselves are very often owned and run by producers. They will often take good wares but generally on a sale or return business. This type of trade often requires you to leave your goods on display for months. If you cannot afford this then you must find other outlets. Gift shops buy certain types of craftware; often they like the items to be small and low in price. They may accept a few more expensive pieces but then they too may require to pay you on sale only. Department stores sometimes have sections selling giftware and you can often actually receive payment from them on normal credit terms. At seasonal times there is often a good trade in suitable items advertised in local papers. One of the best ways to sell craftware is to become accepted in an area. If the public gets used to the idea that a potter or woodworker is beavering away locally, a good trade can start to develop. Sometimes it is worth considering sending your wares considerable distances to find a suitable market — it is always worth researching possibilities of joining together with other producers to do this. Rustic furniture and other country-style woodwork may sell to garden centres and large farm shops. We were talking to the owner of a very large garden centre recently and he said that he was continuously being astonished by the amount of money being spent on garden furniture and ornaments. Although the days of overall high spending have apparently gone, this is an area in which people seem more and more prepared to spend money.

A Victorian Shop

Large Accounts or Small

When it comes to deciding where to base your market, the most visible difference between customers is often the size of orders they will place. The appeal of the large customer is clear: one initial sale and you may be looking at the disposal of a large percentage of your product. In practice the first sale into large organisations is often a time-consuming affair. Usually endless samples are required to go to the different departments concerned with buying a new product. You may be asked to alter your produce to some degree — the packaging or, with foodstuff, the content may have to be altered — to fit in with their market requirements. This can cost a lot of money in real terms and also in other business lost while negotiations are going on. Some large accounts will require you to prove that you have an advertising plan in hand and also to allow discounts to promote the item in low-sales months. The last and possibly biggest danger for the small producer dealing with a large institution is the 'eggs and basket' saga. With a large percentage, possibly all of your produce, going to one outlet, you are in the most vulnerable business position possible. Even if the buyer is your lifelong friend, even if he is your relative, things can change. Jobs change, people change and today seemingly strong companies can go out of business overnight. Unless you have absolutely concrete outlets to fall back on, large accounts must be viewed with extreme caution. The really sad fact about this is that the thrill of selling something you have produced yourself into a customer that may be a household word is immeasurable.

When selling to smaller customers, the immediate problem is that you may need to call on a great number of them to dispose of a suitable quantity. This is where the potential of your product comes into consideration. If the product itself turns over quickly on the retailer's shelves, you can probably get him to take more on the next call. This is where being involved in the business makes sense. You can clearly get alongside the retailer, he will know about delivery costs too and often this common ground makes selling easier. The potential of your customer is also clearly important. If you have to call on a customer who can only ever take a low volume of stock because of his business limitations, it is important to decide if you can afford to make that call. The same time could possibly be spent calling on a better outlet.

Payment terms are extremely important in any business. If you have credit terms on all your supplies or have enough capital to be able to wait, you may be prepared to offer credit. However, the transaction is really only safe when the money is with you. We recently only just avoided losing several dozen jars of mustard from an outlet that went out of business. It was one of the very few customers that we supplied on credit. Fortunately, we heard murmurings the day before they closed and when we amicably asked for our stock back, we were quite amicably given it. This is much safer than waiting forever until someone else decides how much compensation you will be paid. The compensation is often very small if anything; at least this way you can still sell the stock.

A Customised Vehicle

Customise and Advertise!

Distribution to small clients is often a headache. We carry our goods around with us if at all possible and fulfil orders on the spot. Obviously when fresh meat is in question this is not possible; many butchers will, however, order on the telephone once you have proved with a few deliveries that your produce is of a consistent quality. Produce such as jams and confectionery rarely sell well on the telephone. Customers with tourist trade, however, often like to have a telephone number they can ring in an emergency; that is when the whole concept of country enterprise starts off in a life of its own and you find yourself boiling jam and fudge at midnight. Then you are up at six the next morning to label the lot and off to deliver it that morning. We have certainly delivered warm jam to such outlets in the past and it makes the whole concept come alive to the customer.

Advertising

This certainly helps to sell almost anything. There are several different kinds of advertising and often one will work where another does not. We have used word of mouth as a great boost to our direct sales for years. A satisfied pork customer tends to talk about it to his friends: he can talk about the delicious pork he has eaten or he may use some of the pork for a party when again it is talked about. We also hope that our customers enjoy buying from us, coming and seeing aspects of the enterprise in action; hopefully they talk about that too. However, we have just had a clear example of how talking does not always work. Our boxer bitch had a romantic assignation with a local sheepdog and the result was a shock to us and her — six beautiful black and white puppies. We thought they were so beautiful that we would have no difficulty in giving them away. We must have offered them to half of Kent, everyone said how delightful they sounded and that was that. However much we like dogs, seven is too much for anybody so a little desperation set in. A friend then commented that she had sold crossbred pups through the local paper, why didn't we? The response was overwhelming. We were able to select good homes for the puppies and make an excellent profit. In fact, the whole venture went so well that we are quite looking forward to the patter of some more tiny feet!

In some areas, the most effective local papers are the free advertisement papers that are distributed weekly. Some shop-windows are excellent at reaching the public whereas others, often very shiny ones, produce no result at all. At least this latter form of advertising is extremely cheap so you can afford to do some experimenting. When your advertisement is simply one of dozens of similar ones, you may not reach the casual looker so it is worth developing a striking image on paper. Perhaps you can use a drawing of something relevant and a coloured card: this will help your advertisement to stand out from the rest. Your product itself is, of course, an area for advertising. If it is the finest jam you have ever tasted, say so on the label. If the wool you have spun is from your beautiful pet-sheep, Hilda and Meg, then again say so on a label. The public like to be informed: if you have gone to the trouble of producing something special for them to enjoy, someone must tell them about it. The only way you can be sure of this is to make sure that your product carries its own message. Also any product that is used over a length of time, such as the pot of jam sitting on the table every tea-time, will remind your customer of you. If your product is especially good, the customer can then easily remember who to buy from again. This is the theory behind special-brand packs of matches and other similar items. The aim is to keep your name in the public's memory.

Where your product is sold it may be possible to help yourself and the retailer to sell more. Point-of-sale material is often appreciated. We have a poster that many of our mustard stockists display. In fact, it is rarely right beside the product but often finds a place in the window. It can remind the customer that the shop he is entering stocks our mustard; it also points out that the retailer is keen to stock and sell local produce. If you feel your product is one that people would like to order by telephone, you may find an advertisement in the *Yellow Pages* useful: what is often difficult is to decide the category in which you should be listed. It is worth thinking this one out carefully; many would-be purchasers will be lost if they can easily find your competitor but you have disappeared.

When you want the public to come to your premises you will have to put up some kind of sign. For passing trade the sign is the only public image you have. It can attract or repel. We have examples of both extremes near us in Kent. The one that repels is easy to spot. An unbelievably rickety, dirty sign lolls out of a scrubby hedge proclaiming Jersey milk and butter. The thought of untreated milk being produced by the maker of such a scrawled mess is worrying enough. The thought that the milk is further being processed into butter is worse. The appealing sign is a simple black-on-white painted board advertising ducklings, hay and straw and finally table ducks. The sign is always bright and shiny; it is, in fact, taken in when the business is closed and so can quickly be wiped over. It is not too commercial in appearance either. There is a local farm shop that recently put up a sign that would do justice to a superstore. There is no appeal of fresh vegetables in it: the image that springs to mind when this orange monster looms on the landscape is of pre-packed everything. The ideal sign to sell foodstuff is often hand-painted and invariably clean and shining. Potters and woodworkers can run to artistically produced efforts.

Agents

If you do decide to sell through an agent, you will probably find that he has very set ideas about the products he wishes to sell and how he intends to sell them. Agents generally carry several lines. Their whole business is based on the fact that they can offer several lines on every call. Thus they can turn over a high volume of business. You pay a percentage of sales for the agent's efforts. The best kind of agent if you need quick cash flow is a buying agent. This is where the agent backs his judgement by actually buying the goods from you and then selling them on. Most agents do not do this. They sell your goods from samples and then send the orders to you for you to fulfil and deliver. Good agents have one great thing going for them: they are known in the trade in which they work. If they can see your product fitting in with their existing lines, you will probably do very well. There are a great many of another type of agent operating. They are simply trying to pick up a get-rich-quick line. They take your product, with promises of spectacular sales, and then disappear for ever if it is not an instant success. Very few things are an instant success whereas a good business can be built up using time and effort; little effort expended brings no result. We and many people we know have tried using these agents when we have run out of time to practise direct selling. The fact that you have wasted precious time telling them about your product and giving them stock to sell and that you then have to pursue them to get stock back makes the whole episode infuriating.

To employ a full-time salesman is a large commitment. You must be absolutely sure that your production can keep up with the sales you want him to make. It will also take up some of your time keeping your salesman happy. Good salesmen like to feel involved and part of an organisation. They also have to be paid and that is where you really have to justify their employment. There is no point in you working simply to pay your salesman's wages; after all, you must be paid as well. Whoever sells your produce, it is a good idea if you keep a written record of your customers and the amounts they buy. The first reason for this is that this is an easy way to remember who needs repeat calls and when. The other reason is that your customer list is a valuable asset of your business.

Forward Planning

How you foresee your business progressing is an essential part of forward planning. If you intend to keep your production static, you can concentrate on producing and selling in the most efficient way. If you aim to expand the business, you must plan for a different future. If you can foresee the premises you are in being able to cope with the increased production you require, it is also worth considering if those premises would be suitable for sale or transfer at a later date. When your business is established, production is in swing and sales are being fulfilled, you will have created a valuable asset. Whether you can change that asset into money or not depends on where the business is carried out and how. Although today it may seem that you would never wish to sell your enterprise, it is worth having all your options open if you can. A business that can carry on in any premises can be sold for the value of any movable machinery and goodwill. For example, if you are producing fencing, using woodworking machinery and carrying on a regular business with established customers, there is clearly a value in your business. If the enterprise is based on a site that you are able and prepared to sell or lease, the value of the business is increased by more than the straight value of the land. This is because a purchaser is buying a complete, going concern. A potter who produces artistic pieces that sell because of his name and reputation can only sell his machinery and premises. Clearly there is no value in his talent for the purchaser. Bearing these considerations in mind as your enterprise progresses gives you more enjoyment and also provides you with a greater asset.

Note
1. The labels on p. 196 were printed before the Trading Standards Department's advice on this matter!

Finance

A very interesting quote with which to start this chapter comes from John Ockenden, chief information officer at CoSIRA (Council for Small Industries in Rural Areas): 'With the current revival of the traditional rural occupations and the introduction of newer businesses which not only provide employment but also fit neatly into the rural scene, the village is enjoying a renaissance.'

For a country-based enterprise the first organisation to approach for funding would seem to be CoSIRA. They can lend up to £75,000 on their own account and they have links with other lending sources for further sums. They are certainly used to dealing with entrepreneurs working from old farm buildings or farmhouse attics. As well as possibly lending you money they can provide technical and management consultancy. To contact CoSIRA, find them in the Yellow Pages or telephone Salisbury (0722) 6255.

The government's Loan Guarantee Scheme has already helped 10,000 companies to find finance. From the borrower's point of view its main appeal is that it enables an individual, or team, without a proven track record to borrow from sources that would not hitherto have entertained their propositions. It also covers the borrower who does not have adequate security. The government guarantees 80 per cent of the loan made by a participating organisation. The lenders still have to be convinced of the viability of a venture. In fact recently there has been a move towards tightening up the involvement of the borrower, as there have been some instances where proprietors in enterprises borrowing under this scheme have been able to abandon failed businesses leaving others to clear up the resulting chaos.

The clearing banks are able to take advantage of the Guarantee Scheme, although in many cases they still seem more eager to lend on a more usual form of security. Very often a country bank manager will appreciate local conditions of trading, in any case whether he does so or not the first hurdle in borrowing from a clearing bank is to get your manager's support. One way to get a head start is to have your figures clearly presented. Prepare them with the lender's criteria firmly at the front of your mind. A lending source wants to feel that you are totally committed and talented enough to fulfil all the cash-flow projections typed out for his perusal. It appears to be sufficient to scribble a few figures onto a cigarette packet if you want to borrow a few million. It is not if you want a few thousand. *The Financial Times* has produced what it terms the 'First XI' for small businesses. A request for information or assistance to a few of them may well deluge you in paper; a request to them all may well take up so much time that you are unable to pursue your enterprise at all!

FIRST XI FOR SMALL FIRMS

The Alliance of Small Firms and Self Employed People Ltd. 42 Vine Road, East Molesey, Surrey KT8 9LF. Tel. 01-979 2293.

The Association of British Chambers of Commerce. Sovereign House, 212a Shaftesbury Ave, London WC2H 8EW. Tel. 01-240 5831.

Association of Independent Businesses. Trowbray House, 108 Weston St, London SE1 3QB. Tel. 01-403 4066.

Confederation of British Industry. Centre Point, 103 New Oxford St, London WC1A 1DU. Tel. 01-379 7400.

The Forum of Private Business. Ruskin Rooms, Drury Lane, Knutsford, Cheshire WA16 0ED. Tel. 0565 4468.

Institute of Directors. 116 Pall Mall, London SW1Y 5ED. Tel. 01-839 1233.

The National Chamber of Trade. Enterprise House, Henley-on-Thames, Oxon RG9 1TU. Tel. 049-12 6161.

National Federation of Self Employed and Small Businesses Ltd. 32 St Annes Rd West, Lytham St Annes, Lancs FY9 1NY. Tel. 0253 720911.

National Association of Shopkeepers. Lynch House, 91 Mansfield Rd, Nottingham NG1 3FN. Tel. 0620 45046.

The Small Business Bureau. 32 Smith Square, London SW1P 3HH. Tel. 01-222 9000.

Union of Independent Companies. 71 Fleet St, London EC4. Tel. 01-583 9305.

Index

advertising 207-9
agents 7, 209-10
Alpine goats 128
apples 55-7
    recipes 161-4
Approved Woodlands Scheme 67
artificial insemination 132-3
assets 1-9, 210
Aylesbury ducks 114-15
Ayrshire cows 132

bacon 153-6
battery hens 102-3
bed and breakfast trade 140-1
beef 82-5
bees 172-83
    equipment 176-7
    life in the hive 179-81
beeswax 181-2
boars 94-5
bookeeping 8-9
bouquet garnis 53
blackberries 43-4
blackcurrants 41-2
blueberries 44-5
buildings 2-3

calves 83-5
cartons 197
catering 140-4
chamomile 50
Channel Island cows 130
cheesemaking 137-9
    recipes 167-70
chickens 100-11
    rearing 107-9
    recipe 151
chicory 36
Christmas trees 63-4
coarse fishing 191

coconut ice 167
coppice 61
cows 129-32
craft shows 188
cream making 136
crop rotation 19-21
cultivation 16-21, 27-30

dairying 125-39
Dedicated Woodland 66
ditches 27-8
distribution 206
dried flowers 48-9
drop spindle 185-7
ducks 112-18
    breeds 117
    eggs 113-14
    feathers 117-18
    housing 114-16
    meat 114

egg plants 35
eggs 113-14, 115, 120

farm gate sales 8
farrowing 87, 90-3
field beans 21
fish farming 191
flowers 46-9
forward planning 210
fudge 164-7
    creamy 165
    traditional 166

garlic 35
geese 119-24
    eggs 120
    fattening 121
goats 125-8, 137
Goose Breeders Association 123

INDEX / 215

gooseberries 42
grass 10-16
    new leys 13-15
    permanent pasture 10-12
grasshoppers 11-12

hay 13
hens 100-11
    eggs 105
    feeding 104-5
    housing 102-4
    rearing 107-9
    table birds 106-7
herbs 49-54
    salves 52
high forest 62
hives 174-6

Jacob sheep 71-3
Jams 157-62
jars 195

labels 157-9, 196
layers mash 104-5
lemon balm 50
lime 15
loom 186

marketing 194-210
meat 147-9
    pigs head 147-8
    hand and spring 148-9
Milk Marketing Board 126
milking 133-4

Nubian goat 128

organic fertilisers 25-7

packaging 8
pears 57
pigs 86-96
    breeds 89-90
    farrowing 90-3
    runts 93-4

ploughing 16-18
pork 95-6
point of sale 208
portion control 142-3
pot pourri 52
propolis 182

quark 168

rabbits 97-9
    breeding 98-9
    pâté 156
radishes 35
raspberries 37-9
recipes 145-53
    poachers roll 153
    raised pie 149-50
    rillettes 145-7
    sausages 149
redcurrants 42
rennet 168-9
retail sales 143-4
Rouen duck 114
royal jelly 182
runts 93

Saanan goat 128
salesmen 7-8
sea kale 36
seaweed 26
selling 198-207
sheep 67-81
    dairying 129
shooting 191
signs 208-9
silage 14
Small Woods Scheme 67
smoking 155
soil 24-5
sows 94
spinning 187
strawberries 39-41
swarm 177-9

Toggenbergs 128